"At a time when the publishing world appears writing, author and editor Windy Lynn Harris stands out—an easy-to-read, no-nonsense compendium of original wisdom on the art and science of short prose. Unlike many other volumes on the market, *Writing & Selling Short Stories & Personal Essays* offers insights into two related but distinct challenges—writing successful stories and essays, and marketing those works once they are written. The book abounds with first-rate advice and draws upon numerous practical examples. Harris clearly has mastered the distinct crafts of writing and publishing—and she can help you do so too. If you're only going to buy one book to launch your career as a writing professional, this is the book." **—JACOB M. APPEL**, author of *The Mask of Sanity*

"Better pick up several copies, because you will be handing them out to friends and students. Windy Lynn Harris's *Writing & Selling Short Stories & Personal Essays* demystifies the process of writing and publishing short form writing with refreshing clarity and ease. There is something here for writers of every skill level and experience. Harris's professional experience as a published author, editor, and consultant shine in this guide. Her patience and knowledge emerge from the pages as though you have a mentor to assist you along the journey." **—APRIL BRADLEY**, writer, editor, and Pushcart nominee.

"Windy Lynn Harris has succeeded in writing a thorough, engaging, easy to understand 'how-to' bible for the writing industry. It's chock full of great writing samples, templates, and clear instructions on both craft and marketing. There is something for everyone in this book; both the novice and the published writer will gain much from studying these pages. I, for one, will keep a copy close to my desk, no doubt dog-earring pages and re-reading Harris's sage advice again and again." **—ALICE KALTMAN**, author of *Staggerwing* and *Wavehouse* (2018)

"Windy's book, *Writing & Selling Short Stories & Personal Essays* is a practical and user-friendly guide to add those coveted bylines to your resume. Each section of the book breaks down what you need to know to garner success in your writing career." **—RUDRI BHATT PATEL**, essayist and co-founder/co-editor of *The Sunlight Press*

"Finally! A straightforward guide to polishing, formatting, and publishing essays and short stories. Windy Lynn Harris demystifies the process and makes it easy to navigate the path to publishing. This book will have a permanent place on my desk." **—SUSAN POHLMAN**, essayist and author of *Halfway to Each Other: How a Year in Italy Brought Our Family Home*

"This gem of a book is chock full of helpful tips and advice for writers who want to break into the short fiction and/or essay market. Along with detailed advice on the craft of writing short stories and essays, you will also find databases and resources for publishing your polished work. *Writing & Selling Short Stories & Personal Essays* is a must-have for every writer's bookshelf." —**JEANNE LYET GASSMAN**, author of the Independent Publisher Book Award-winning *Blood of a Stone*

"Writers, here it is—the one book you need to start your journey to writing and publishing. Windy Lynn Harris, herself a seasoned writer, is your sure-footed tour guide who teaches you the language of the locals. Part MFA professor, part cheerleader, and always your trusted mentor, Windy draws on her own experience as writer and writing coach to demystify the craft and process of writing and publishing short stories and essays. Beginners can rely on this book to teach them everything they need to know from the basic structure and scope of short stories and essays to where and how to publish them. Seasoned writers will learn more than a few new tricks of the trade. The numerous top ten tips alone are worth the price of admission. Though there are many books on craft out there, and others on publishing, this book is truly your one-stop shopping!" —**JENNIFER KIRCHER KARR**, co-founder of WordTango and winner of the *Nebraska Review*'s Fiction Prize.

"Rooted in the context of the current short-form literary landscape, *Writing & Selling Short Stories & Personal Essays* is more than an excellent source of information. Each page is the best kind of companion—one who helps you out while also cheering you on. Functioning as both a craft book and an informative guide, Harris's unique collection helps us first to find the most succinct way to put our experiences and ideas on the page, and then how to get our words out into the world. I'm not quite sure how anyone has been able to write effectively in the short form genre prior to this book's existence." —**CHELSEY CLAMMER** (author of *Circadian* and *BodyHome*)

"*Writing & Selling Short Stories & Personal Essays* is a brilliant and concise guide to writing compelling work and getting it published. From sharpening the implements in your creative writing toolbox, to crafting a perfect cover letter, and identifying the best markets for your work, Windy Lynn Harris delivers expert advice for every stage of the process. When it comes to writing short work and getting it published Windy tells her readers 'you can do this,' and with her book you will!"—**ELIZABETH PETTIE**, co-founder of WordTango

Writing & Selling

SHORT STORIES

&

PERSONAL ESSAYS

WINDY LYNN HARRIS

WRITER'S DIGEST
BOOKS

WritersDigest.com
Cincinnati, Ohio

For more resources for writers, visit www.writersdigest.com.

21 20 19 18   5 4 3 2

Distributed in Canada by Fraser Direct
100 Armstrong Avenue
Georgetown, Ontario, Canada L7G 5S4
Tel: (905) 877-4411

Distributed in the U.K. and Europe by F+W Media International
Pynes Hill Court, Pynes Hill, Rydon Lane
Exeter, EX2 5AZ, United Kingdom
Tel: (+44) 1392-797680, Fax: (+44) 1626-323319
E-mail: postmaster@davidandcharles.co.uk

Library of Congress Cataloging-in-Publication Data

ISBN-13: 978-1-4403-5083-2

Edited by Cris Freese
Designed by Alexis Estoye
Production coordinated by Debbie Thomas

DEDICATION

For Darin, always.

ACKNOWLEDGMENTS

I relied on a large tribe of family and friends for support during the year this book was written. I had a neck injury, months of physical therapy, spinal surgery, and a recovery period among the drafts of this project. I'd like to thank my husband, Darin, for his enormous contribution to my well-being. There were many days when I was unable to write (or open the refrigerator), but Darin never once worried that I wouldn't finish this book. He didn't let me worry about it either. Thank you, D, for always believing I'd find a way back to the page. Thank you also to my son Jason and my daughter Tierney for their humor and support through the ups and downs of my progress and for lifting all the heavy stuff for me.

A huge thank you to Stuart Horwitz at Book Architecture, who was part of this project from the beginning. Stuart urged me to put my idea down on paper and helped me organize it into a book proposal worth sending out to the world. He was my first beta-reader and a crucial editor along the way. I'm grateful to have you by my side!

Thank you to Rachel Randall at Writer's Digest Books for seeing potential in this material, helping me refine what I could offer writers, and championing this project to print. Thank you also to my literary agent, Julia Kenny, who understands how important this book is to me and ushered it to the finish line. To my terrific and talented editor Cris Freese: Thank you for using that very sharp red pen of yours and for wrangling the organization of this material into a cohesive book. I picture you in the jungle with a machete, but that's probably not how you dress for work at all.

A special thanks goes to Diane Amento Owens for supporting this project way back when we were presenting workshops together at Barnes & Noble. Thank you for believing in me all those years ago and nudging me toward my goal as the years marched on. To my Storytelling Boot Camp partner and dear friend Lisa Fugard: Thank you for igniting the teaching side of my writing life. You make everything seem possible.

A huge thank you goes out to Jennifer Fabiano, Susan Pohlman, and Rudri Bhatt Patel, three amazing writers who served as manuscript beta readers for this book. These friends offered advice at every turn and directed me toward better drafts. Your support means the world to me, ladies.

To Bree Barton, Denise Howard Long, and Brianne M. Kohl: You're the best critique group ever assembled. Thank you for reading chapters of this book along the way and pointing me toward my authentic path. I cherish each of you individually and adore you collectively.

Finally, I would like to thank each of the talented writers and editors who contributed advice, anecdotes, stories, and essays to this book. Every writer needs a tribe, but I've been especially lucky in the company I keep. Thanks goes to each of you for offering time and energy to this project. Your generous advice will help other writers find their way to success, too.

ABOUT THE AUTHOR

Windy Lynn Harris is a prolific writer, a trusted mentor, and a frequent speaker at literary events. Her short stories and personal essays have been published in literary, trade, and women's magazines across the United States and Canada in places like *The Literary Review, The Sunlight Press*, and *Literary Mama*, among many other journals. She is the founder of Market Coaching for Creative Writers, a program that teaches writers how to get their essays and short stories published in magazines, and she works as a developmental-editor-for-hire, specifically for short creative prose. Windy also teaches the craft of writing online and in person. Visit her website for publishing information and writing inspiration: www.windylynnharris.com.

TABLE *of* CONTENTS

PART ONE:

Writing Short Stories & Personal Essays

PART TWO:

Selling Short Stories & Personal Essays

INTRODUCTION

Writing short stories and personal essays is a marketable skill in publishing. These types of short pieces are submitted and accepted every week. And the great news about this kind of writing: Writers don't need a literary agent to participate in the process. We can independently market our prose and land bylines that make us proud. It just takes sending our work to the right editor, at the right time, and in the right way.

In 2009, I founded the Market Coaching for Creative Writers program to help writers get their short stories and personal essays published in magazines. In that program, I teach writers how to create targeted cover letters, professionally format their manuscripts, and find hundreds of perfect markets to match their voice. They study magazine guidelines and submission etiquette, learn the difference between copyright and the rights available to sell, and set up a system for keeping their submissions organized. By the end of a Market Coaching session, writers are not only able to submit their work to viable magazine editors with confidence; they're able to repeat the process for every piece of short writing they produce in the future.

Writing & Selling Short Stories & Personal Essays is going to teach you all of those things, too and more. This book is a complete conversation on the topic of publishing short works.

The first part of this book is dedicated to storytelling because we must create the best version of our prose before reaching out to magazine editors. To learn how to recognize sharp prose, we'll start by examining contemporary short stories and personal essays. Then we'll study voice, scene writing, setting, characterization, point of view, meaningful dialogue, and theme. We'll discuss how to craft publishable short stories and essays and how to revise them effectively.

All of these topics will likely be familiar to you already, but in this book we'll study them through the tightly focused lens of short-form writing. Every craft chapter is specifically designed to help you excel in economical storytelling. You'll learn to pay attention to every single detail.

The second half of this book is a complete guide to getting your work published. You'll learn the five steps to submitting short prose and how to stand out from the crowd. You'll learn how to market yourself before you have any writing credits and how to showcase yourself as an experienced, published writer. You'll even learn how to become a larger part of the literary community. By the end of this book, you'll know how to cultivate relationships with magazine editors and how to put together a support team of like-minded writers.

You won't be alone on this journey. I've invited along published writers and journal editors to share their advice and anecdotes in these pages. These wonderful people have gifted their best tips, biggest regrets, and true stories of publishing success.

My hope is that you read these pages and know you aren't alone when you submit your short work. You are part of a wonderful community of writers and editors who want to see you succeed. We want you to write what's in your heart and then submit your work for the rest of us to read.

Now, let's get to work; shall we?

Part One

WRITING SHORT STORIES

&

PERSONAL ESSAYS

DEFINING THE SHORT STORY

Before we look at the building blocks of great storytelling, I'd like to talk about contemporary short stories and personal essays. We'll start with the short story. A short story is a short work of fiction. Many of the same craft techniques used to write novels are used to write short stories, but the short story stands apart as a separate form of prose—one delivered with concise language. The use of compression and microscopic storytelling makes short stories unique. A short story isn't a chapter from a book but a *complete* experience delivered in a small package.

Besides length, short stories are unique because the action usually revolves around a single dramatic event. It is a *glimpse* of a character's life—perhaps one year or even one hour. Every moment in the story is a dance between action and reaction that is related to a single dramatic event. These stories begin as close to the main conflict as possible, giving an unmistakable immediacy to the prose.

Short stories can be enjoyed in one sitting, but that time frame varies from story to story. Short stories can be as simple as six words or run eighty pages long. Most short stories published today fall somewhere between one-and seven-thousand words, but longer stories and shorter stories can still find homes. There is no hard rule to follow with word count.

The terms "flash fiction" and "microfiction" refer to the very shortest of stories. Microfiction is a story that tops out at one hundred words. Flash fiction is anything between one-hundred to one-thousand words. Anything above one-thousand words (and up to twenty-thousand words) is simply called a short story.

....

"One common definition of flash fiction is that it is a complete story in fewer than one-thousand words. But I dislike this idea of flash fiction as merely a very-condensed short story. I believe strongly that it is its own unique and fluid form. The most exciting flash fiction I have read—and I have read a great deal—is what's been published in recent years. New writers particularly have taken the form and run with it, innovating and experimenting and stretching the boundaries of storytelling. With a limited number of words at the writer's disposal, flash fiction lends itself well to playfulness, form-bending, risk-taking. And the results are thrilling.

Having said all this, though, the flash-fiction story still needs to "work" on some level, right? Absent a template or hard rules, what defines a successful short short story? I believe it is the presence of three necessary elements: emotion, movement, and resonance. A flash-fiction-length story can succeed without one or more of these, but it cannot, in my opinion, be truly great without all three."

—KATHY FISH

....

Well-written short stories are highly desirable pieces of prose. There are plenty of markets to place this type of work. You'll find short stories in literary magazines (*The Literary Review*, *Black Warrior Review*, *Passages North*, etc.), genre magazines (*Ellery Queen Mystery Magazine*, *Asimov's Science Fiction*, *Lightspeed*, etc.) children's magazines (*Cricket*,

Highlights, Ladybug, etc.), and commercial magazines (*The New Yorker, The Saturday Evening Post, Reader's Digest*, etc.). Some are even sold as digital shorts on Amazon or other digital retailers.

I mention the caveat "well-written short stories" because even though there are many outlets for short stories, the competition to earn a space on the pages of a journal is quite stiff. For any writing project, you must create, revise, and polish your work until it meets the standards of the market to which you're submitting, and in the world of short stories, that standard is skyscraper tall. Short stories are some of the most clever, experimental, urgent, and fresh prose being written today.

Part of the reason is the long-respected history of great storytellers and their iconic short stories, such as Raymond Carver's "Cathedral," Ernest Hemingway's "The Killers," Flannery O'Connor's "Greenleaf," and William Faulkner's "A Rose for Emily." I could go on for quite some time before running out of names, but the point I'm making is that short-story writers still aspire to equal the masters. This category's authors and publishers will always hear the echo of notable writers in the distance. So today, editors search for contemporary yet barrel-aged stories that have been given enough careful crafting to mellow into greatness.

WHAT IF MY STORY IS MORE THAN 20,000 WORDS LONG? WILL IT EVER GET PUBLISHED?

The answer is this: probably not. And definitely not as a short story.

This super-long short-story problem happens during some early drafts, and it might mean that you have a lot of editing ahead of you but perhaps not. If you are writing a short story and you're still going strong forty pages in, you might actually be writing a novel instead. There's always a climactic story moment waiting in the distance when you're writing, but you never know how far away that moment is until you actually finish your story.

Along the way, if you see interesting subplots forming, you're heading into novel territory. And if you've developed immediate hurdles for your character along with a big-picture problem, you're probably writing a novel then, too.

Conversely, if you're stretching out scenes or narrative passages for no purposeful reason, you are probably advancing a short story's plot at a sluggish pace. Unlike novels, short stories do not have room for meandering. They require the use of compression and tight scenes. Think you might have this problem? Take a look at one of your key scenes. If you can cut it down by a quarter or more, do it. Then tackle the rest of your story the same way.

GET TO KNOW SHORT STORIES BY READING

Reading short stories is a great way to absorb the concept of condensed prose. There are many styles of stories being published today. Each journal has a unique aesthetic. Reading a variety of different magazines will help you understand what the current literary landscape looks like, and it will also help you see which ones publish work that is similar to yours.

You can find short stories online and in print at various literary journals. Several short-story writers have also published collections of their stories. I like to buy the *Pushcart Prize: Best of the Small Presses* anthology each year because it showcases stories from several different magazines.

To get you started, I've gathered some stories here as examples of what is being published in journals today. The first story is a piece of flash fiction by Kathy Fish called "Düsseldorf." I chose this story because it's a terrific example of the three dramatic elements of flash stories that Kathy mentioned earlier: emotion, movement, and resonance.

DÜSSELDORF
by Kathy Fish
Published in *Yemassee* 23.1.

I have not left the room in three days, and the maids are impatient to clean it. [*From the first sentence, the mood is set.*] It's October, and my husband has brought me along on his business trip. We've been to London and Paris. Now we are in Düsseldorf, and the sun never shines.

I keep the drapes closed, order room service, nibble kuchen under the eiderdown. The room smells like rotten apples. [*The emotion is clear by the end of this first paragraph: Loneliness pervades everything.*]

There's an art museum somewhere. I could take a cab or walk to the museum, or I could lunch by the river. According to the map in the guidebook, we are not far from the river.

In Paris, in a smoky brasserie, my husband spoke at length about his client. He said she is smarter than any man and young but wise and savvy.

"I hate the word savvy," I said. "And all women are smarter than men. It is no great accomplishment."

When he talks to her on the phone, his voice changes register, as if he's been told he's won a major prize. I wonder what she looks like.

The maids pound on the door again. I go into the bathroom and lock the door. I can hear the rattling of keys, their stout, German voices.

The bathroom door knob turns back and forth. I wait for them to give up and leave me in peace.

"Frau? Frau?"

There's nothing to it. I open the door, smiling, grab my sweater and my bag with the guidebook and an umbrella and leave them to the clutter.

There are no people on the street. It's Tuesday, the middle of the day. I walk a long ways. I turn corners and stop, forgetting which direction I came from. Nothing looks as it ought to. The gray and brown buildings stretch to the clouds.

I find a bench and flip through the guidebook. I don't recognize anything from the pictures. All the streets appear the same. Only chestnut trees. Only plain, boxy buildings. Maybe I should return to my hotel. Lying on the grass, not two feet away, I see a dead squirrel.

A little boy in wire-rimmed glasses comes towards me. He's eating a sandwich wrapped in foil. I ask him if he speaks English.

"Yes. I speak English," he says, around the bread and cheese.

"Good. Can you tell me where we are?"

He laughs and says, "This is the city of Düsseldorf." He offers me the rest of his sandwich. I decline.

"But where are all the people? Where are the birds? I haven't heard a single bird chirp or a dog bark. Where are the cars, the streets signs?

If this is a city, where are the shops, the cafés, the restaurants, the bars? Where did you get that sandwich? Who makes the music and the art? Where are all the feral cats?"

The boy chews his sandwich and swallows.

I sniff the air. "Why, I can't even smell anything, can you?"

"Düsseldorf is a beautiful German city on the Rhine River. Its population is eleven million," he says.

"I don't believe you."

The boy crumples the foil into a ball and throws it at my face. He tears off down the sidewalk.

Maybe the squirrel is only sleeping, but I've never seen a squirrel sleeping out in the open. It seems a risky thing for a squirrel to do. Early in our marriage, my husband brought home a rescue dog. A border-collie mix. We named him Rex. He mostly sat in the corner of the laundry room, chewing his paws. Gradually, Rex came to trust us, and we took him everywhere with us. He slept between us, licked our faces until we woke up. One day he simply disappeared. [*The line about Rex the dog changes the story completely. It illuminates the narrator's fear. It's the movement moment of this short piece.*]

The guidebook says that Düsseldorf is a city known for its fashion. If I can find a shop, I'll buy my husband a tie. I'll buy him a hundred ties in every color and drape them over our bed. I walk the streets for miles, but there are no shops and no ties. For one crazy moment, I imagine Rex bounding towards me, like: "There you are; I've been looking all over for you!"

Over the tops of the buildings, the moon rises. I am alone, and Düsseldorf is empty. I stand in the middle of the street with my arms raised, calling my husband's name. And it keeps coming back to me, over and over, like a verse. [*This resonant ending is perfection. We feel the narrator's heartache. We understand that she is the one who is lost.*]

This next example is a story by Alice Kaltman, who is a master at delivering a complete experience in a small amount of space. Her story, "Freedom," feels like a novel, though it's only seven pages long

FREEDOM
By Alice Kaltman
Published in *Luna Luna*, January 2015

Republished in the collection *Staggerwing* in 2016

Oh, the burn. That searing pain squeezing his thighs like a vise grip. The supreme feeling. The most validating. Even more affirming than the heaving sensation in his gut. A smaller gut these days. But still a paunch, folded over burning thighs as Danny pedaled fast and furious through the Vermont countryside.

Danny had never been a big one for physical pain. But the past few months had changed that. Now he was a glutton for punishment, as long as it came via two wheels, multiple gears, and a padded seat. Biking had become his thing. It might smack of mid-life crisis, but no question, it was a healthy outlet. Much better than a trophy wife or sporty car. Not that either of those were viable options for an overweight New York City public-school English teacher recently dumped by his high-power-executive wife.

The super-steep Vermont inclines provided pure bliss. Now another magnificent hill was coming his way. Danny shifted expertly to proper gear. Like the little engine that could, he made his way to the top. I think I can; I think I can. …

****

Four months earlier, [*Kaltman's use of setting up a moment and then stepping back in time precludes the need to begin with boring backstory. She already has us invested in the main character. Now we're hungry to find out why this man is pushing himself so hard.*] on a tepidly overcast April afternoon, Danny trudged like a tired refugee towards the subway. Meg had planted the bomb two weeks earlier. Her actual words: "It's not working, Danny. Our fighting is bad for Cody. You know it, and I know it. I want a divorce." The subtext: "I'm having the best sex of my life with Craig Gundersen. I'm not that interested in the whole parenting thing. I'm out of here, you fat fuck."

No question who Cody should end up with as far as Danny was concerned. What the courts decided was another matter.

Before descending the subway stairs, he lifted his eyes momentarily, hoping for a glimmer of sunlight, a ray of something akin to hope. It was then Danny spotted the bike, propped in the window of Urban Cyclist, front wheel slightly elevated, as if to create the illusion of flight: the Kestrel Talon. Maybe it was the name, the implication of speed and slice. Or maybe it was how the weak sunlight reflected off the bicycle's silver metal while it barely warmed Danny's disappointed soul. The Kestrel Talon gleamed. It downright beckoned. Danny hadn't ridden a bike in fifteen years. The damn thing set him back two-thousand bucks.

He trained every day. Got up at five A.M., headed to Central Park and did the loop, not just once, not just twice. By mid-May it was often ten times. Danny added extra workouts in the afternoons, snuck out of MS 115 like a cat burglar, skipped the useless faculty meetings, let his perpetually delinquent students off without detention. Why waste his breath?

All rides were cathartic, his earliest ones pointedly so. Danny's cycling was ferocious, if uncouth and energy inefficient. His pre-divorce imagination went vividly wild. Danny rounded the 110th Street hill and left a long tar-and-pebbled gash across the sloping asphalt which he fantasized was Meg's formidible ass. The downhill at 72nd Street provided opportunity to hyper-speed along the delicate bridge of Meg's lovely nose. Danny broke it, deviated her septum. Snap, snap, snap. Ah, but the sweetest musing of all came at the southeast corner of 59th, where Danny pumped his brakes to gouge a repeated pattern along the meat of Craig Gundersen's overrated cock.

****

[*These breaks in time move the story along at the pace necessary to deliver a story in seven pages, no extra scenes or narrative passages here. Kaltman barrels us toward the next important story moment.*]

Now it was August, with only a few niggling details of shared custody to work out. Danny had arrived at this remote corner of Vermont two days earlier with the Kestrel Talon secured to the roof of his Prius. He checked in to Olaf's Country Inn, an old farmhouse with a few musty spare rooms near the back entrance. Tomorrow uber-parenting would begin again. Danny would be sitting in the outdoor Arpeggio Lake Music Camp Amphitheatre, trying to covertly swat voracious mosquitoes while his brilliant flute prodigy of a son trilled his way through Mozart. Last year Danny and Meg had come together, sitting closer to each other than they had in years all for Cody's benefit. Meg would've rather died. She complained about the heat, the uncomfortable back-less outdoor seating, the bugs, the humidity, the other parents. But it was Danny she most abhorred. Danny with his hairy, clammy thigh pressing against her wall of impenetrable smoothness.

But this summer, Danny was in biking heaven. Meg was out at Gundersen's East Hampton compound doing God knew what. Danny couldn't care less. He was in stellar cycling form. There was no more need for revenge riding now that he was such a cycling beast. No decline or coasting or resting before he got to the tippy top of this hill. Just. Going. For. The. Burn.

Hill, meet Danny. Danny, meet Hill.

He crested the top and gave himself a silent cheer. No pause, just an easy coast down, taking in the sights. Danny passed beauty; he passed despair. To his left, gold flowers sprouted through the broken window of a derelict home. Vines with deep purple blossoms twisted around yellow hazard tape on a rusted wire fence. To his right, a gorgeous green field was filled with abandoned car chassis. If Danny still wrote poetry, this contradictory Vermont landscape would provide inspiration. Better than teaching slow-witted eighth graders to churn out their own half-baked verse, that was for sure.

Danny hit a straightaway. Time to pour on the juice. He looked at the speedometer. Forty mph. Not too shabby. He couldn't help wondering if Craig Gunderson was capable of such a feat. But why think of such things? Danny refocused. Speed was his priority.

There was a minor obstacle just ahead, before another magnificent hill. A dog straining on a chain connected to a stake at the end of the straightaway. Imprisoned on a dusty patch of earth at the foot of a beautiful incline. Another countryside paradox. It looked like a mutt. But what did Danny know about dogs? He'd never owned one. His childhood had been petless. His Depression-era parents had had no extra cash floating around their Flatbush apartment to feed a mouth that wasn't even human. Cody, of course, had always wanted a dog. But Meg was allergic, which was lucky, because Danny was a wee-bit scared of dogs.

But Vermont dogs were tolerable, in large part because they were always behind fences, roped to mailboxes, leashed to barns, or chained to posts like this one. They were shackled, while Danny was free.

The dog edged its front paws onto the asphalt. Toenails click-clacked like castanets as it lurched and howled. It was female, emaciated but with a bunch of droopy teats.

Danny grunted as he did a clean little loopy loo around the poor, hapless beast. He moved onward and upward. The hill was mighty steep. Danny's breath was shallow. His gut lurched. His heart pumped. And joy of joys, his thighs were killing him! Perfection but for the continued, desperate yapping of that dog down the hill.

At the summit, Danny stopped to take a swig of Powerade. He took big gulps of the fresh Vermont air and told himself he was glad to be alive. He gazed behind himself, proud to survey where he'd come from. The dog stared up at him, quiet now. She knew her limits.

"Top o' the mornin' to ya, Ma'am," he called to her with a jaunty and terrible faux-Irish accent.

The dog barked once. Then, with canine decisiveness, she bounded up the hill at quite a clip, the chain and upended stake clanging behind her like tin cans attached to a newlywed's bumper.

Danny scrambled to reattach his cleats, his entire body quaking. He adjusted his gears, and after a wobbly start, he careened down the next decline. His breath was shallow. His gut lurched. His heart pumped. But this was panic, not joy.

The dog raced closer, dragging that damn stake and chain. She was fast for a scrawny little thing.

Danny willed himself to focus on the road ahead. The dog was gaining on him, galloping like a horse. She was so near, Danny could hear her wheezing breath. There was a gurgle and a catch to it. The dog was determined. Maybe desperate, too.

The pothole was an unforeseen conclusion. While Danny flew over his handlebars, he thought, *Who will cut the crusts off Cody's peanut butter and banana sandwiches?*

He landed with a dull thud. Bruised and scraped but nothing severed. His extra poundage had cushioned the blow. Before he could get up, the dog was upon him, her paws pressed against his chest. She licked his cheeks, his lips. She slobbered all over his bike goggles, his helmet, his neck.

Her collar was so tight that her dun-colored fur puffed and swelled around it. Yellow crud coated her lower lids. Her breath was swampy and hot. The dangling teats were dried up, crusted over, spent. Danny lay still and let the dog kiss him. There was no need for any more fear. Eventually he reached up to unbuckle her collar. Underneath, the bare doggy skin was red and raw. She paused for a moment, registering this new sensation, breeze on flesh. She sniffed the air, considered the empty road ahead. Then she returned her gaze to Danny with eyes dark as tar and started kissing him again.

Danny rolled out from under her. Instantly she leaned in to him, her ribs pressing against his sopping-wet tunic. Olaf's Inn was less than a quarter mile away. An easy ride. An easy run. There were no other guests. And there was that back entrance after all.

Cody had always wanted a dog.

"Do you know how to keep quiet?" Danny asked.

The dog looked up at him and blinked. [*The reader has witnessed Danny cycling his way back to self-worth. We are also aware of the bigger picture—the new kind of life he wants to have with his son Cody. Bonus: He's got room in his heart for a dog now, too.*]

This next story is from Denise H. Long. "Dollhouse" is a perfect example of the unmistakable immediacy of short stories. Her use of concise language and compression in every paragraph leave no extra words on the page.

DOLLHOUSE
by Denise H. Long
Published in Matter Press's *Journal of Compressed Creative Arts*, January 2017

From her mattress on the floor, the girl tries to block out the noise from downstairs, the music, the glass breaking, the laughter too loud for anything to have been funny. The sounds that sometimes push past the lock of her bedroom door and the dresser she pushes against it, hunting for her in the tangle of blankets that used to swallow her whole. [*There are two clever moments in this story that tell us this girl has been here for a long time. She's grown up in this room, which no longer fits her—literally and figuratively.*]

But as the night grows darker, the girl turns out her lights, unfolds herself, and climbs into the small wooden house in the corner of her room.

She slides aside the tiny staircase and the miniature couch with matching side chairs. She stacks the end tables on top of each other and balances them atop the coffee table. She moves the beds to one side, careful not to disturb the family that lies under handkerchief blankets, each member touching another. And she pulls her legs underneath her, curves her back to the slope of the roof, stretching into the pinches of what might no longer fit. [*This is the second hint that this girl has outgrown her surroundings.*]

She runs her hands over her skin, blooming with delicate hives, finding intricate patterns in her scabs. She feels the gentle teeth of the bugs in her unwashed hair, waiting for them to settle into the crevices behind her ears, imagining it's their voices that echo in her head.

As she tucks her chin to her chest, she waits for morning, when the darkness will bend and break, letting in the cool light of day. And she will pull her fingers free from the grate of the tiny windows and dig her toes into the soft wood of the house's floors. She will touch the family's impossibly tiny smiles and wish herself smaller, fit for of their world. [*In this last sentence, we feel the truth of a much larger story. The girl wants to escape back to a better time in her life, but she sees the impossibility of it.*]

This last short story is from me, titled "Mrs. Anderson's Jesus." I've included it here as an example of the dance between action and reaction, all relating to one single dramatic story event. In this case, the event is a storm that brought notoriety to one small town.

MRS. ANDERSON'S JESUS
by Windy Lynn Harris
Published in *Pithead Chapel*, December 2015

There was a dust storm in Duval that September, during the single driest month the town had ever recorded. Harsh winds became mini twisters that tore across cotton fields and baseball parks. One of those dust devils knocked over a cow. One ripped the "Welcome to Duval" sign clean off its post.

And one of them brought Jesus to Mrs. Anderson's front porch. [*The story begins as close to the main conflict as possible.*]

Painters working on Mrs. Anderson's railing had to abandon their jobs when a swirl of dust crossed main street and spun right into Mrs. Anderson's yard. The men dropped their brushes and ran into Mrs. Anderson's house, leaving the open paint cans to the will of the twirling wind. Hunter-green and lemon-yellow globs flew up and out, splattering Mrs. Anderson's home.

"Stop right there," Mrs. Anderson barked. She admonished the men for taking it upon themselves to rush into her home. Not one of them had wiped his feet.

"The wind," the foreman said, hands in the air. "It attacked us."

"Nonsense," Mrs. Anderson said.

The wind had died down enough for the men to feel foolish under the scrutiny of their client. "Please forgive us," the foreman said. He motioned for his men to head back outside, but all three of his employees hesitated. The foreman had to open the door first to prove it was safe. When he did, green and yellow globs dripped down the door and onto Mrs. Anderson's polished entryway.

Mrs. Anderson shrieked. "What have you fools done? You've ruined my door!"

"We'll fix it; I promise," said the foreman. He hurried the other men out and used his hands to stop more paint from dripping. "Hand me those paper towels and a tarp," he said to the open door.

Nobody answered him.

"Hurry!" yelled Mrs. Anderson, watching the circles of paint begin to harden on her floor, but still, not one employee came back.

Mrs. Anderson stomped to the door and peered past the foreman. She saw all three painters on their knees. "You idiots!" she cried. Mrs. Anderson pushed the foreman into the wet door as she passed him. "Can't you hear your boss? Don't any of you boys obey?"

The three men ignored her, shaking their heads in disbelief. She walked up behind them, and that's when she finally saw it, too, the face of Jesus in a blend of yellow and green against her once-white front wall. The Son of God was quickly drying in the hot sun, smiling right at Mrs. Anderson.

"It's a sign from God," [*Up to this point, we've seen small action and reaction moments: The dust devil comes up on the porch, which makes the men run inside; Mrs. Anderson shoos them back out. With the appearance of Jesus' face, the action and reaction moments escalate.*] she announced, and the men nodded. The foreman came to the porch, too and gasped. Mrs. Anderson swelled with pride.

Neighbors soon came to inspect the miracle, and all who saw it concurred. It was Jesus all right, and nobody was more pleased than Mrs. Anderson. She'd been avoiding her church ever since her sister had taken Mrs. Anderson's place as the leader of the choir, stealing the spotlight with her trumped-up ideas about fairness and taking turns at the top. Jesus Himself must have been upset about it, too, Mrs. Anderson decided. He'd practically shouted his opinion across the front of her house.

Mrs. Anderson basked in the new awe of her neighbors. She nodded at her Jesus, thanking Him for choosing her. She silently made a pact with him. Mrs. Anderson promised not to let her greedy sister Beatrice get in the way again. Beatrice had already ruined the choir with those flashy red satin robes. Who knew what the woman would do to Jesus Himself? They'd be dignified, this paint Jesus and she, and discerning about sharing God's mission.

The town clergy came around within the hour. Reverend Frank shook Mrs. Anderson's hand and blessed her right there on her front porch in front of the growing crowd. She closed her eyes demurely and accepted the Reverend's praise. It was even better than an apology.

Soon the Lutheran pastor came and the Catholic Deacon, too. The three holy men studied the blobs and drips, each seeing their own nuances in the paint. Pastor Gold saw Jesus' full robe and sandals in the paint below his face, right where Deacon Merr saw a hundred-year-long beard. Mrs. Anderson thought they were both wrong and tried to share a knowing look with Reverend Frank, but he was distracted with his own interpretations.

Mrs. Anderson invited the clergy to sit on her comfortable porch chairs while they drank her homemade lemonade. She thawed a container of snickerdoodles for them on her best china plate and presented the cookies with a newfound piety. She'd intended to bring the snickerdoodles to the choir meeting when they asked her to return, but so far,

Beatrice had kept the singers from calling. That was about to change, Mrs. Anderson thought as she watched Reverend Frank take his first bite. She'd gladly bake another batch for her homecoming.

The next morning, people showed up from all over town and crowded themselves onto Mrs. Anderson's lawn. She had to shoo a few of them from her front porch, and before the three town clergymen returned, she'd been forced to tie a garden hose across her stair rails to keep the rest of the gawkers out. When the men finally arrived, Reverend Frank was too distracted to notice how perfectly matched she and her Jesus were, even though Mrs. Anderson had posed beside the miracle in her best yellow blouse as the men ducked under the hose and joined her on the porch. Reverend Frank asked her about coffee instead. The men settled into their now-familiar spots on her furniture and waited to be served. Mrs. Anderson hurried, eager to rejoin them. She'd had an idea about a lawn sign declaring the significance of her property last night. Reverend Frank would want her church to sponsor it, she was sure. Even Beatrice, who'd traveled to hungry countries helping the poor, hadn't ever been blessed by Jesus Himself. Maybe there should be a shrine.

When Mrs. Anderson brought coffee out to the men, they were nearly shouting to each other over the noise of the swelling horde. The crowd had doubled in her minutes away. Mrs. Anderson couldn't see a blade of her own grass under all those feet. Women kneeled in her flowerbeds, murmuring their prayers. A man on crutches leaned against her mailbox and chanted in a foreign language. A baby wailed loud enough to be heard over them all. Mrs. Anderson fought the instinct to clap her hands together and hurry them away, reminding herself that she was hosting a miracle from God. She'd have to endure some sacrifice.

And that included Beatrice, who was right that moment trying to duck under the garden hose.

Mrs. Anderson waved her sister back before she could barge onto the porch. She slipped under the hose herself and joined her sister on the other side of it. She pulled Beatrice to the edge of her yard, away from the important trio discussing her Jesus.

"It's a miracle, Aggie!" Beatrice gushed, hugging Mrs. Anderson too tightly around the neck. "We're saved!"

"It is a blessing," Mrs. Anderson agreed. She nodded her head thoughtfully and worked on a humble smile.

"Everyone is so excited! The whole town is coming. It was on the radio!"

"Is that so?" Mrs. Anderson let a smile escape. "I would have called you, but I've been so busy here."

"No worry. We've come to help. The ladies and I have taken care of everything." Beatrice clapped her hands three times. "We're setting up in the driveway."

Mrs. Anderson puckered at what she saw behind her sister. Long tables were already dressed in white cloth with potluck dishes lined up in a row. Two men pulled stacks of folding chairs out of the back of a pickup truck. "What's all this?" Mrs. Anderson asked.

"The whole town is buzzing, Aggs. The drought will be over soon!" She grasped her sister's hands. "We've been praying for this all month."

Beatrice planted a wet kiss on her sister's cheek, then bustled back to the driveway, leaving Mrs. Anderson to absorb the rest of the scene. Cars jostled past each other down the block, vying for the last parking space. Neighboring yards swelled with people. A brown-eyed girl asked to use her bathroom.

"Find your mother!" Mrs. Anderson snapped. "This isn't a carnival." [*At this point, the action and reaction moments become desperate, further escalating the tension all the way to the climax.*]

Mrs. Anderson hurried back up to her porch. The town's newspaper photographer had crept through her barricade and was snapping shots of the clergy in front of her Jesus. Mrs. Anderson inserted herself into the frame next to Reverend Frank, but it was a moment too late. The photographer had just called, "Done." The men returned to their chairs and asked Mrs. Anderson to bring a fresh pot of coffee.

She did refill their cups, but she left the brownies she'd made that morning on the counter in her kitchen. Mrs. Anderson parked herself in the chair next to Reverend Frank and tried to regain her footing. This was, after all, her property they were all so excited about.

The Jesus painting was a sign from God, the church leaders agreed, but it wasn't until lunchtime when the national-news crews arrived that they formed a united opinion about it. "Jesus has come to Duval to send a message of peace," Reverend Frank told the cameras. He spoke to the vast crowd from the railing of Mrs. Anderson's front porch, with the hostess shoved far off to the left. "We are all God's children," he said and motioned to the crowd with open arms.

People cheered and pressed forward. Mrs. Anderson saw Beatrice slip up the stairs, a spectacle in her red choir robe. "It's so exciting!" Beatrice said, winding an arm around Mrs. Anderson's waist. Mrs. Anderson bristled but kept her smile tight in case the camera had a wide enough angle to include them.

"Come and pray with us tonight," Reverend Frank said. He clutched a Bible to his heart. "We're holding a candlelight vigil. We'll stand together and sing to our Lord!"

A rush of heat marched up Mrs. Anderson's neck. She refused to look at her smug sister. She nodded along instead. "Yes, of course," she said. "We will sing." Mrs. Anderson saw a flash of red near her driveway and turned to watch the rest of the choir zip themselves into their hideous new robes, too.

Reverend Frank had the church ladies fussing with Mrs. Anderson's porch for the rest of the afternoon, stapling cheap streamers to her railing and paper flowers in a rectangle shape that framed Jesus' face. They replaced her deck furniture with the church's wooden pulpit and placed eight folding chairs in a row under her Jesus. Beatrice set songbooks on each of the chairs, humming "Let There Be Peace On Earth," but it may as well have been a victory song. There was no place for Mrs. Anderson to sit.

In that moment, Mrs. Anderson formed a plan. She looked her Jesus in the eye and knew He agreed. Sacrifices would have to be made.

Swarms of people came to Mrs. Anderson's lawn that evening, holding tall white candles and trampling her begonias. They pressed themselves right up against her railing. Mrs. Anderson stood at the edge of her own porch with a lit candle in her hand, wondering why the choir members each had one as well. They'd be clapping to the rhythm, if Mrs. Anderson was still in charge, but Beatrice had made so many foolish changes it was hard to keep track. Reverend Frank quieted the crowd and began his sermon with the Lord's Prayer. Mrs. Anderson mouthed along with the crowd. Beatrice and the other singers were a garish spectacle of red against the backdrop of her Jesus.

Mrs. Anderson waited until Reverend Frank was to the part of his presentation where he stepped into the crowd to offer his blessings by placing his palm on the forehead of the lucky parishioners nearest him. Desperate people cheered and begged Reverend Frank to come farther into the crowd. During a brief rehearsal, Reverend Frank had told the choir to stand near the front of the porch while he did this and sing "Thou Art a Savior." The women now swayed and belted out their song for all to hear, dripping wax on Mrs. Anderson's fine wood.

When the hymn began its second verse, Mrs. Anderson made her move. She crept behind the choir and touched her candle to the nearest paper flower. Her Jesus would have winked if He could. Mrs. Anderson nodded a goodbye before slipping back across the porch and down the stairs.

Beatrice was the first to see the flames, but her screams and gestures were drowned by the revelry and song. She pulled the rest of the choir off the porch before the last of the flowers lit up. Screams rippled through the crowd then, and all eyes watched as Mrs. Anderson's Jesus was swallowed by flames.

A man ran to the porch with a fire extinguisher in time to save Mrs. Anderson's home, but it was too late for Jesus. The fire had blackened His face to an unrecognizable smudge. "No!" cried Beatrice. She was the first to run back onto the porch. "He'd come to save us!" Beatrice stood in the glow of Mrs. Anderson's porch light, arms back, screaming to Heaven.

And that's when Mrs. Anderson saw it. She covered her mouth and didn't dare point to her sister's red choir robe, in case she was the only one to notice, but one by one the crowd dropped to their knees in silence. Mrs. Anderson's curse shot like a cannon across the quiet yard.

Reverend Frank walked slowly toward Beatrice as she herself looked down at the reason the mood had changed. Mrs. Anderson's sister pointed to the white wax that had splattered across her robe in the commotion. Even she could see the perfect outline of the Virgin Mary's delicate face. Reverend Frank knelt in front of Beatrice and took her right hand. "It's a miracle," he said. [*This last action and reaction moment echoes the beginning of the story and wraps up the original dramatic event.*]

DEFINING THE PERSONAL ESSAY

Personal essays are appealing first-person stories often found in magazines and newspapers. They're true stories told by people willing to share their intimate thoughts and feelings about life. They are incredibly popular, with plenty of submission opportunities for writers.

These stories are nonfiction, but they stand apart from other nonfiction pieces because of their purposeful use of storytelling. We're not talking about self-help, how-to, or informative articles, which all require the writer to slip into an invisible narrator's voice. Essays bloom well beyond that informational tone. Well-written essays harness cadence, individuality, a narrative arc, and creativity.

Studying the craft of writing is essential to creating publishable personal essays. Writing the truth is important, but great storytelling holds equal weight. Personal essays have rising tension, compelling characters, and mini-plotlines that push the reader toward a conclusion or a realization. A personal essay isn't simply an anecdote but an in-depth exploration of a subject.

Essay categories include travel, parenting, grief, humor, satire, nostalgia, divorce, friendship, personal growth, and much more. Essays can cover a trip with your mother-in-law to Las Vegas or a midlife moment in the mirror. They can explore the injustice of racism or the beautiful healing nature of butterflies. They can be filled with hope, anger, or angst. Essays have that delicious inclusion factor that grabs readers by the heart and makes them feel something.

Personal essays whose style strongly emphasizes literary elements (symbolism, setting, style, tone, theme, characterization, etc.) find homes in literary magazines like *Tin House, The Sun, The Paris Review,* etc. Reported essays—an essay that contains a personal narrative with some degree of reporting and statistical analysis—are found in news sources and lifestyle magazines like *The Washington Post, Aeon, The Guardian,* etc. All other essays, including well-written prose with any degree of literary emphasis, are found in nearly every other print and online publication.

Many places that publish personal essays will state clearly that they are looking for creative nonfiction. Creative nonfiction is an industry term that includes literary essays along with other creative nonfiction, including travel essays, parenting essays, and pieces of inspired reportage, among other things. Outlets looking to acquire creative nonfiction are advertising, essentially, that they publish personal essays on a variety of topics that contain a large amount of *scene development.*

The key to well-written creative nonfiction is in the use of scenes to convey the story. Creative nonfiction essays use less narrative and more scene-by-scene storytelling—a technique that pushes the sensory experience for readers. When readers feel the action of an essay, they can make inferences, judgments, and emotional connections. They can experience the events with personal investment. Readers can then examine their own experiences in comparison.

Creative nonfiction is the fastest-growing area of nonfiction, with opportunities for writers in magazines and newspapers across the country. The genre allows for experimentation in a way that appeals to readers of fiction and nonfiction alike. Not every magazine is looking specifically for creative nonfiction, but if that's the direction your work takes you, know that you will have many opportunities for publication.

Author Susan Pohlman has written creative-nonfiction essays for a variety of print and online outlets. She likens these essays to fiction, in terms of technique: "Creative nonfiction is an umbrella term. It is an easily accessible genre encompassing a multitude of forms such as the personal essay, the profile essay, participatory journalism, memoir, features, travel essays, biography, and inspired reportage on almost any subject. In short, creative nonfiction is the art of applying storytelling techniques to nonfiction prose. They are true stories that read like fiction."

That's right—they read *like* fiction. Don't let that confuse you. They feel like fiction because they employ such a big dose of scene development, but creative-nonfiction essays are all accurate depictions of people's lives. They are true stories crafted to elicit an emotional response.

THE DIFFERENCE BETWEEN ACADEMIC ESSAYS & PERSONAL ESSAYS

Academic essays (also called argument, stance, expository, position, thesis, or claim essays) use research and evidence to support an idea. The author is an objective observer during the research process and expresses the results by way of a formally written essay. The structure of academic essays begins with an introduction, then leads to the body of the work, and finishes with a fact-based conclusion. The intention is to present even-handed consideration of an issue through logical and rational thinking.

Personal essays, in contrast, are developed through life experiences, opinions, and meaningful moments. Personal essays are pieces of self-expression shared through prose. They are based on true events, seen through your eyes, and felt by your heart, a subjective account or opinion on a specific topic or event. A personal essay is guided by your emotions, gut feelings, and worldview—but it's much more than a journal entry. Personal essays explore the moments in life that change us. The intention is to connect with readers in a universal way.

If you have written an academic essay on a subject that goes beyond the interest of your colleagues, you can still find a home for it in the world of personal essays—with some work. First, step back from your topic and subjectively reevaluate your material. How does it make you feel? Is there a universal message somewhere that you've learned along the way? Did the completion of your thesis research create a meaningful moment in your life? Ask yourself: Am I willing to reveal my own personal feelings about this subject? If the answer is yes, keep reading. Your academic essay might be the inspiration that leads you to write a terrific personal essay.

GET TO KNOW PERSONAL ESSAYS BY READING

The best way to understand the look and feel of a contemporary personal essay is to read a selection of published pieces. You'll find many different styles and a variety of subjects. With study, you'll gain a sense of where your own voice fits into the mix.

Every year there are several essay anthologies published. My favorite is *The Best American Essays*. They compile the top essays from magazines across the country. The book showcases how a publishable essay reads, and you also get a sense of what the editors of each magazine consider their best work.

I've selected a few of my favorite essays here to get you started in your study. This first essay is from Susan Pohlman. "A Mother's Silhouette" is a terrific example of creative nonfiction. Pohlman keeps us in one room throughout this piece, even as she wanders through drowsy memories.

A MOTHER'S SILHOUETTE
by Susan Pohlman
Published in *The Mid*, June 2015

I awoke for a moment in late afternoon, the hospital room spare and efficient. I looked over and saw my mother sitting with a rosary in her hand, a cool dark silhouette before a window fiercely illuminated by the hot desert sun.

"You don't have to talk," she said, noticing I was stirring. "I'm just going to sit here."

Thank you. It's exactly what I needed. An immense, familiar peace filled me, her profile eliciting early memories as I continued to drift in and out of sleep, my body ridding itself of the anesthesia from an early-morning surgery.

I dreamed of sitting tall beside her as she drove the white station wagon with two sure hands on the wheel down bright summer streets and squinting up from my canvas raft to see that she still sat in the striped beach chair in case I needed her to rescue me from the crashing waves. Then I was suddenly spinning on the old, brown Naugahyde-covered stool in the kitchen as she prepared dinner, her black wavy hair in sharp contrast to the fading glare of a snowy afternoon through windows over the kitchen sink. I felt the weight of her as she perched on the edge of my bed, saying prayers with me, the hall light streaming behind her into my room cloaked in night. Her slight frame in the living room window as I pulled up to the house in an old blue Ford with my first boyfriend.

All of these memories, backlit, glowing. A mother's silhouette. [*This image heightens the awareness of a mother sitting nearby throughout the author's life.*] Anchoring, soothing, solid. As an adult, going about the daily routines, I had forgotten about the calming, restorative effect of having my mother simply sit in my presence. I looked to her as I always have. My mirror, my friend, my ever-present reminder-er that my haircut is all wrong and my weight is too low. All these years she has been the constant in my life. Now sneaking around the edges of my heart is the knowledge that she will someday be gone. It is an unbearable knowing. Where will she be when I need her? Who will be backlit for me then?

The ability to have children may end, but mothering endures. It is a singular and beautiful calling to become the silhouette to love's light here on this Earth. In this room, helpless and still, I saw clearly that my position in the chain of motherhood would remain unchanged. A child doesn't stop needing his or her mother simply because he or she is growing older, and a mother's instinct to love her children never ends.

My thoughts turned to my son and daughter, young adults trying to find their way and make sense of their circumstances. I wonder if my silhouette holds the same power. If I was there when they needed to peer from their own darkness and look toward the light. If I understood when they were young that love shines brightest during the simple moments of mothering that become so routine that we perform them without thought.

I look forward with a new understanding to the many years I have left with them. Even if that means just sitting in a chair in a shadowy room by a sunny window, a chance to remind them of the immense, familiar peace of a mother's love in this often harsh world.

I awakened again, [*Here is where Pohlman brings us back into the physical scene, but we feel like we've been here all along.*] my head pounding. She was there in a second with ice chips and a cool cloth. "Do you want me to turn off the ceiling light?" she asked as she leaned over me.

"No, leave it on," I replied, adding one more image to my treasure box of silhouettes.

Sheets smoothed, pillows adjusted, she stood searching for some other detail to attend. "Thanks, Mom," I said as I felt the tug of sleep once more.

"I'll just sit over here," she whispered. "You don't have to talk." [*Pohlman has purposefully bookended this piece with these words from her mother, giving a sense of closure to this essay.*]

This next essay is from Bree Barton. "The Greatest Lesson We Learn When Someone Is Unkind" is a wonderful example of interiority. Barton meets a compelling character, and their exchange prompts self-evaluation.

THE GREATEST LESSON WE LEARN WHEN SOMEONE IS UNKIND
By Bree Barton
Published in *Tiny Buddha*, November 2013
Reprinted in *Tiny Buddha's 365 Tiny Love Challenges* (New York: HarperOne, 2015)

I recently travelled to Malaysia for a friend's wedding. The people were kind and warm, the culture rich, the trip magical. On my last day in Kuala Lumpur, I was headed out to buy souvenirs for family and friends when I stumbled across the most beautiful temple. I wandered around, overcome with majesty, trying to breathe it all in. I was still under the temple's spell when someone spoke to me.

"Your dress is ugly."

I looked to my right where the voice had come from. A woman was sitting on a bench, not looking in my direction. "Sorry?" I said, thinking I must have misheard.

She waved me off. I stood there for a moment, trying to decide on a course of action. She was American, the first and only other American I'd met during my trip.

Had she really just said my dress was ugly? *Maybe she said my dress was pretty,* I thought. I must have misunderstood. [*This passage of interiority reveals the surprise and confusion Barton felt.*]

"Did you just say my dress is ugly?" I asked.

"Yeah," she said. "I did."

I took a deep breath and replied, calmly, "Why would you say that to me?"

"I'm entitled to my opinion," she said. "Your dress is ugly; I can tell it's not well made. Your purse is dirty. I am free to voice my thoughts, and those are my thoughts about you."

To say it felt like getting slapped in the face would be an understatement; it was more of a punch to the gut. My blood boiled, my heart raced, but still I kept my voice at an even keel. [*We see the inner struggle escalate.*]

"You are entitled to your own opinion," I said. "But we also live in congress with other human beings. Why would you say something so aggressive and unkind?"

She reiterated her insults. Her words sliced coolly into the way I looked and the clothes I wore. That's when I said the one thing I regret saying.

"I wish there were fewer Americans like you traveling abroad," I told her. "You give the rest of us a bad name." [*This is the end of the exchange but not Barton's interiority. The essay continues to move forward as the author ponders this woman and what it means to be unkind.*]

I turned and walked away, and she yelled one more barb at my back as I walked out of the temple. My hands were shaking as I walked down the street. I felt a strange knot of emotions in my chest: hurt, anger, fear. Why did this woman choose to attack me? Why had she said what she said?

I had just read the wonderful convocation address given by George Saunders to the Syracuse class of 2013. George talks about something he calls a "failure of kindness," and those three words were very much on my mind. Yes, you could say I had suffered from a failure of kindness. But what I realized was that I, too, had been unkind.

I wish I hadn't said what I said to her. That came from a place of being wounded, of feeling the need to fight back. I wish I had said: "I hope the people you meet are kind."

Because I do hope that for her. I hope that she is bathed in loving-kindness, that she is inundated with so much that she cannot help but share it with the world.

While it's true that kindness engenders kindness, the lack of it can be a powerful teacher. For my remaining hours in Kuala Lumpur, I was abundantly kind to everyone I met. I complimented a girl on her joyful spirit, told shop owners how beautiful their merchandise was, smiled widely and genuinely. I made a point to be kind to these warm, generous people who had so kindly shared their country with me.

And every time I was shown kindness, no matter how small, I felt immeasurably grateful. That woman gave me a great gift. She reminded me that we all have a choice to be kind, and we are presented with that choice many times a day. [*Barton's theme is presented beautifully in this last line of interiority.*]

Next comes an essay from Rudri Bhatt Patel. "The Mother of the House" is a short literary piece where the featured action is a woman cooking bread at the stove—but the essay stretches miles beyond that moment. It is an expansive essay told in very few words.

THE MOTHER OF THE HOUSE
by Rudri Bhatt Patel
Published in *Brain, Child: The Magazine for Thinking Mothers*, January 2015

My mother tells me that she doesn't know what home is anymore. I sigh, not wanting the words to land. [*Patel sets up an interesting mother/daughter conflict with hints of their history in only two sentences.*] She sits at my dining table, while I make her fresh *roti,* an Indian bread that I devoured as a little girl. Her hands lay in her lap, and her half-smile reflects her ambivalence. I notice her veins, the bright blue lines laying roads on her arms.

"I don't get it, Mom. What do you mean? When you are with family, it isn't enough. You also complain that your apartment feels lonely. Which one is it?" I flip the round *roti* on our stove, my elbows awkward and displaced as I try to save the bread from burning. She tries to explain. "When you lose your companion," she says, "there is no place that fulfills you. This is my new normal after Dad's passing."

I feel the weight of her words and my mouth opens, but the words are stuck. Instead I watch as a piece of the bread burns at the edges.

"It is too late. There is nothing to save." [*These lines of dialogue jar the narrator and change the tone of the piece, escalating the tension. The lines have two meanings here: It's too late to save the man they are mourning, and it's too late to save the bread (which represents the present).*] My mom interrupts my thoughts as I toy with trying to save the *roti*.

For a minute, I am confused. I am unclear whether she is talking about her loneliness or the bread. The conversation about her displaced home occurs, almost on repeat, every time my mother and I intersect. She confesses her pendulum of discontent. I reply in silence.

I accept that this is her new voice. The voice of a widow mourning the loss of a life she keeps referring to in the present tense.

What I didn't expect is how much I've started to mother my own mom. [*This simple sentence allows readers to imagine the other ways these women's roles have changed. It expands the essay beyond this moment in the kitchen.*] I am a forty-something raising my eight-year-old daughter and taking care of my mother, too. When my daughter comes home from school, I ask her those familiar words that resonate in cars all over the country, "How was your day?" Sometimes she replies with a boisterous response; other times I plead with her to confess at least one detail. When I ask my mom the same question, she will often respond with a single-word answer, and like a good "parent," I keep prodding her until she reveals that her stomach hurt at night and she didn't get much sleep. [*The reader and Patel accept the new normal. The roles have been reversed.*]

This next essay is from travel writer Lynn O'Rourke Hayes. In her piece, "An Eddy In Time," Hayes explores the idea of *letting go* during a fishing

Writing & Selling Short Stories & Personal Essays

trip with her grown son. The essay is universal in its topic and is made individual by Hayes's outdoor adventures—both past and present.

AN EDDY IN TIME

by Lynn O'Rourke Hayes

Published in *The Huffington Post*, November 2012

Fly rod in hand, I eased into the warm waters of the storied Madison River. [*Hayes leads us into her world, and the mood is set.*] My son, Ben, was just steps behind me, eager to wet his line. Despite my felt-bottomed shoes, I faltered slightly, slipping off the rounded, moss-covered rocks below my feet.

"Here, take my hand," Ben said softly behind me. "I'll help you."

Steadied by his strength, together we pushed forward, bolstered against the rippling current.

At 6'3", my oldest son towers over me now. This should come as no surprise. Mothers with children older than mine had long presaged it would happen like this; a fast-forward blur of growth spurts, sporting events, back-to-school nights and prom dates. But really, wasn't it just yesterday that I took his small hand in mine and walked him into preschool? And just last week that I steadied him on skis as he slipped down a snowy pathway during a family ski holiday? And now, some twenty years later, he is holding me upright as we wade into these braided waters under the wide Montana sky. [*This is an essay about recognizing her son is grown, accepting that he is an adult.*]

This was more than a casual weekend. He had called to suggest we meet for a few days of mother-son fly-fishing, an interest we have shared since his boyhood. Our destination would be the mountains and rivers of Big Sky country, a landscape we both love. After, we would both head to Northern Idaho for the big event. In just seven days, he would wait at the end of yet another pathway to catch that first glimpse of his beautiful bride.

Throughout the weekend, we fished favorite streams and crossed canyons via zip line, joking about the next "big leap" he would soon take. We walked through the woods with his two golden retrievers, Bridger and Jackson, and reminisced about our family life. We both ordered curried chicken for lunch and lamented our mutual metabolism that required us to leave the banana bread at the counter, particularly now, the weekend before the wedding.

I wondered if there wasn't something important, something meaningful I should say. Some kind of prenuptial, motherly advice I could offer. But it wasn't required.

Someone asked if I felt that sense of loss some women suffer, a heart-splitting notion that marriage somehow meant losing your son to another woman. For us, there is none of that. I know that I will always be his mom and she will always be his girl.

Each evening we retreated to our room at the Big Sky Lodge, curled up with the dogs, reviewed the day's events, and planned for the next. We shared our individual enthusiasm for the upcoming wedding festivities. I smiled with deep pleasure when he spoke with confidence of his decision to marry Lyndsay and how special and strong he believed their relationship to be. There was no hesitation. Only eager anticipation.

From time to time, I would catch glimpses of a much younger Ben. [*Hayes braids the boy and the man brilliantly.*] A familiar, silly grin. A childlike glance in a moment of indecision. But mostly, I saw a sure-footed man, eager to embark on this next chapter of his life.

On our last afternoon, we made one more stop along the Gallatin, hoping to improve our luck. While we both knew this weekend wasn't just about the fish, a little more action would have been welcome. Once again, Ben provided a steady hand as we waded into the water. As the sun dropped behind the cliff and soft evening light prevailed, we took turns casting, attempting to lure the wily trout from its safe hideout.

At one point, my line became hopelessly entangled. Without hesitation or frustration, Ben quietly took my rod and said, "Not to worry. I can help." It's what I might have whispered two decades ago when he fell off the jungle gym or scraped his knee in a Rollerblade spill. [*Hayes points out their changing roles.*] But now, somehow it seemed just right that he would be the problem solver, the one to take the lead.

As the weekend came to a close, he said, "Mom, your baby boy is getting married. Can you believe it?"

What I believe is that time mysteriously evaporates and in the blink of an eye, that once mischievous toddler strides back into the room as a confident, young man. A man insightful and caring enough to create this eddy in time, in the scant hours before dozens of friends, family, and a long list of last-minute details would vie for his attention.

Knowing he has become this measure of a man provides soul-satisfying comfort. I am certain he will be a fine husband and father, locking arms with his wife through rough waters and calm seas. He'll be present when their child takes that first shaky step, hesitates on the first day of school, or ties the first fly.

And with this knowing, I will shed tears of pride and joy as he reaches for the hand of his lovely bride, closes his own around hers, and before family and friends, promises to love her and hold her steady. For always. [*This last line resonates with trust and happiness.*]

This last essay is from Lisa Fugard. In "Here A Bushbuck, There A Crane," the author revisits South Africa, and as she does, she is brought back to morning drives with her father, "through the kingdom of the animals" to the "world of Irish nuns." As the essay evolves, Fugard realizes that those early drives set her on a lifelong journey.

HERE A BUSHBUCK, THERE A CRANE
by Lisa Fugard
Published in *The New York Times*, September 1999

I was driving along the R572 between Messina and Pontdrif when I spotted the large blackbreasted snake eagle perched on a telephone pole. I braked, reversed, and stepped slowly out of the car so as not to startle it. I used my binoculars for a moment, out of habit, and then put them down. There was something about looking through them that made the eagle seem as if it were in a separate world. [*Fugard tells readers right up front that she wants to be close to the creatures she meets along her journey.*] It wasn't. Barely twenty feet of hot asphalt separated us.

In a game reserve, I might spend two to three minutes looking at such a bird and then move on in search of larger game, but when I'm driving the small dirt and tar roads of South Africa, any animal sighting, no matter how humble, feels like a privilege.

I quietly eased myself onto the trunk of my car and watched the eagle. Wind ruffled its black feathers. In its talons I noticed a large bloody hunk of something scaly—lizard or snake. The eagle scanned the landscape and periodically glanced at me with eyes that were a piercing yellow.

I often think about those eyes. I want to say that the eagle looked at me with utter detachment, but that doesn't quite capture the sense of mystery I felt while spending half an hour with that animal. [*The author is fascinated, and the reader feels it, too.*] The more I stared at that eagle, the more unknowable it became. Who needs encounters with aliens when there are animals on this Earth?

My delight in these poor man's safaris, as I call my modest backroad adventures, goes back to my childhood in South Africa where I grew up and in particular to early-morning drives to school with my father.

We lived near Port Elizabeth, and the road to St. Dominic's Priory led through a stretch of coastal bush on the outskirts of the city. A short drive for an adult—only twenty minutes—but for me, when I was young, it was a passage through the kingdom of the animals before I entered the world of Irish nuns, arithmetic, and ABCs.

My father and I often encountered troops of vervet monkeys. We moved tortoises off the road and saw the occasional bushbuck. In early spring, when somnolent puff adders and cape cobras sought the warmth of the tar road, we stopped for snake rescue. Most South Africans drive right over snakes; my father tried to save them by skillfully ushering them back into the bush.

Not every drive, however, offered such simple joys. One morning we found a fatally wounded bushbuck on the road. I waited in the car, crying, while my father and the motorist who had accidentally hit the buck struggled to end its life.

By the time I reached my moody teenaged years, it was second nature for me to look for animals on the side of the road. [*Fugard smoothly moves through time in her memory with this line.*] Long drives to our holiday home in the dreaded Karoo (a vast semidesert region that occupies much of the Western and Eastern Cape interior, not the greatest hangout for a fifteen-year-old girl) turned into more opportunities to see animals. Desperate thoughts about boys nicknamed Bristles and Mouse would fade as I stared out the car window. Yes! Springbok grazing in the distance. Baboons scrabbling into the bush. Wow! Three blue cranes at that dam.

It took leaving South Africa at age eighteen and then returning to visit a decade later for me to discover the great game reserves of the country and, on subsequent visits, those of Botswana and Zimbabwe. I've galloped away from lions while on a horse safari, canoed through a gantlet of hippos, and walked silently through the bush to view a breeding herd of elephants, yet I still feel luckiest when I stumble upon animals during my back-road explorations.

These days, as I grow more aware of the vulnerability of animals outside protected areas, there is an added poignancy to each encounter. [*There is a reverence for animals throughout this piece.*] "Jackals are vermin, so why not run them over?" seems to be the approach of some people. Crop farmers and baboons are sworn enemies, and until recently sheep farmers shot eagles. A few years ago, monkeys in the bush near Port Elizabeth were found with their hands chopped off, the work of an African herbalist.

My most recent poor man's safari took me though the far reaches of the country's Northern Province, a scorchingly hot land where the monotony of miles of mopane scrub is broken by conical termite hills and eerie baobab trees. Roadside sightings in this part of South Africa tend to involve slightly larger animals.

During one nighttime drive, I spotted a caracal, an animal that's rarely seen, even in a game reserve. The long tufted ears were a giveaway. I braked and reversed just in time to watch the elegant golden cat slip into the night beyond my headlights.

Driving into Pontdrif, the border post between South Africa and Botswana, I encountered my first bat-eared fox, lying dead outside the house of a police officer. While I studied the huge ears of the fox, the police officer, a gentleman devoted to putting an end to the poaching in the area, explained that he'd found the fox dead on the road that morning. He took it home to study it and maybe even have it mounted; he was interested in taxidermy. Electric-green flies crawling over the body told both of us that it was too late for that; the fox had already begun to decompose.

"Look out for cheetah," the police officer said to me when I left Pontdrif late that afternoon. "I've seen them sitting in the road." I took the R521 south and drove slowly. I scanned the tangle of bush beyond the roadside fences, but after twenty miles I'd seen no wildlife of any kind. Not my lucky day, I thought, and I picked up speed.

And then, just north of Alldays—a miserable, sweltering little village with a cheap hotel, taxidermy shop, mortuary and butcher—I almost collided with a cheetah. Suddenly there it was, a flurry of spots and the most extraordinary long legs unfurling across the road in front of me. I slammed on the brakes, just in time to see the animal crouch down and whip beneath the fence on the opposite side of the road, its long tail trailing behind like a billow of silk scarf.

I whooped and cried and thumped the steering wheel for the next five miles. Then I noticed an African fish eagle on a dead tree next to a small dam and a family of antennae-tailed warthogs scuttling into the bush. I was still in the kingdom of the animals, and it was dusk, close to the hour when a black-backed jackal might dart across the road ... [*Fugard ends this essay with renewed excitement. She is filled with possibility.*]

3

VOICE

We hear the word "voice" a lot in appraisals of writing. The term can be confusing. You might hear, "Aden's voice is just so original!" or "The voice of this piece really punched me in the gut." These are terrific compliments, but what exactly is voice? Most commonly, voice refers to how a writer's unique word choice and syntax reflect her worldview, identity, or personality. So if someone tells you that your writing has a strong voice, he is expressing his appreciation for the singular stylistic fingerprint imbued in your essays/stories.

You've probably already got your own personal narrator voice—and practice will only improve it.

THE TOOLS OF THE TRADE

Your authentic voice can shine with a combination of diction, the details you select, images, syntax, and tone. Let's take a closer look at each of these elements and how to use them like a pro:

- **DICTION** refers to your choice of words. Words affect the reader's experience when they are chosen with purpose. For example, instead of saying *house*, consider using the word *mansion*, *cottage*, or *Victorian*. Each of those words has a unique connotation. Consider the different effect you can create when you refer to a person as *vain* and when you refer to someone as *proud*. The word *vain* assigns a negative connotation to this person, while the word *proud* might reflect the same character traits but in a much more positive light. You can choose to be poetic, vulgar, literal, formal, or anything else in your prose and show it to your readers via diction. If you intend to entertain, choose playful words or an ironic combination of words. When you want to persuade, use straightforward, confident language.

- **DETAILS** include the facts, observations, and specific moments you choose to share in your story or essay. You can enhance the reader's experience by choosing concrete details. For instance, *a dented red Mustang* is more descriptive than *a car*. Details encourage reader participation. Each word creates an opportunity for the reader to fill in the physical world he sees in your prose. You can also manipulate the reading experience through the number of details you include. When you use a handful of specific details in a paragraph, the reader leans in, gets closer to your story. When you use fewer details, the reader will feel a distance.

- **IMAGERY** adds an extra layer to your prose through sensory details. These sensory details evoke a vivid experience for the reader. The tools at your disposal are the five senses: sight, smell, sound, touch, and taste. Using these, you can trigger pleasant or unpleasant emotions, create confusion or surprise, or be provocative—all through your choice of images.

- **SYNTAX** is the order of your words, which creates the rhythm of your piece. You can manage this effect by varying your sentence length. Short sentences speed up momentum. Long ones slow down the action and let readers closely examine scenes. Repetition of certain words can also be an artistic choice.

- **TONE** reveals your underlying attitude toward the characters/people and situations in your writing and your story's/essay's subject matter. Are you angry? Sad? Apologetic? Somber? Whatever your feelings about your topic, let your readers know. Tone is achieved through the combination of your diction and syntax and is emphasized through the details and imagery you choose. Readers perceive your tone by examining these elements. They connect to the material and its underlying meaning via your attitude.

....

"Developing voice as a writer is about finding the courage to be yourself on the page. The secret to understanding voice is revealed when you watch and listen to a child at play. Children express themselves without self-critique. They are who they are without apology. Feelings and observations bubble up and out naturally. Delightful and endlessly entertaining, they observe and interpret the world around them according to their God-given natures.

"As writers, we need to peel away the layers of life and cultural restraint to rediscover this pure essence of ourselves, to learn again to delight in and observe the world around us without apology, according to our authentic selves. Readers want to read you, not you trying to sound like another writer."

—SUSAN POHLMAN
....

YOUR VOICE RIGHT NOW

Your voice becomes more evident as you create a body of work to examine, but you can still study even a few of your written works for style clues. What you're looking for is that uniqueness only you bring to the page. Is there a cadence to your sentences that repeats? Do you use metaphors regularly? Are there poetic phrases within your prose? Do you develop common themes?

Check your voice every year or so, and study your evolution. Compare a recent story you wrote with one from a year ago. What about your writing has improved? Are your essays becoming more complex? Are your stories layered with deeper themes? What do you wish was more refined?

This might sound like you're doing an inventory of your writing skills—because you are. The more you understand about the craft of writing, the better you can apply that knowledge to your stories and essays. This, in turn, affects a market's desire to publish your work. Don't worry if you have trouble identifying your style. With time, you will create a strong voice. Keep writing, examining, and growing in your craft.

How to Study Voice Through Reading

One of the best ways to learn the intricacies of your own voice is to study the voice of other writers. Studying the individuality of a writer's style helps us identify what "having a style" looks like; it assists us in discovering our own voice. Let's take a close look at voice and examine it on the page. I've chosen excerpts from three different published first-person short stories. You only need a page—or sometimes only a paragraph—to get a sense of a writer's voice.

The first short story, "The Half Dollar," is by Denise H. Long, who has a knack for character dialect. Her story is a terrific example of diction and tone working side by side.

(excerpt from) **THE HALF DOLLAR**
by Denise H. Long
Published in *Blue Monday Review*, January 2016

It had only taken my sister Roberta one time of trying to keep a bit of her five-and-dime wages to realize Pop meant business. My sisters and I never had any money of our own. Pop said any money earned was family money.

But I *found* that half-dollar, which is different, I think. What happened to it was up to me. I was walking home from school, and there it was, lying on the ground in front of Fletcher's General. I saw Benjamin Franklin's face staring up at me, glinting in the sun. Nobody was nearby. I'd seen Rufin Tomasik backing his dad's ancient Model T runabout moments before, the relic tied together with leather straps and a prayer. The coin could've been his, but he was long gone. So I pinched it from the dirt.

Heavy in my hand, the large metal surface dwarfed my palm. It was the most money I'd ever held that didn't belong to somebody else. I tilted it back and forth, watching the sun bounce off Franklin's bald head, winking. Like Pop would say, though, "With possibility comes responsibility," the long syllables rolling off his tongue right before he spat in the empty coffee can Mama cleaned every day and left by his chair.

I thought of going into Fletcher's right then and there. Plunking the half-dollar down on the counter. Watching Lainie Fletcher's eyes bug out when I tell her to fill up one of their little brown bags with Turkish taffy and cherry lumps and then taking my change home with me to keep. But I didn't want change. I wanted my half-dollar intact. Whole and heavy in my hand.

Notice Long's clean and direct writing style. Her diction is informal. She gives hints of small-town innocence through words like *Pop*, *pinched*, *dwarfed*, and *plunking*. The glinting half-dollar becomes something much more than a piece of money to the little girl. It is a symbol of her struggle in the world. Long puts this symbol on display and shines a light so bright that we can't look away.

The second story is from Brianne M. Kohl, whose use of detail stands out on the page.

(excerpt from) **RHONDA'S FITBIT FIELD NOTES**
by Brianne M. Kohl
Published in *Literary Mama*, April 2016

I am mired in a room with a yellow glow. We painted the walls Lemon Twist and decorated in accents of gray, green, and brown. It sounds ugly, but it isn't because of all the teddy bears. I sit on the floor with my son, Ryder, as he hands me toy after toy: teething rings and stuffed-animal rattles and the occasional brightly colored rubber block. He smiles with his little baby teeth, tongue twisting around the nubs. We have matching plump bellies and cankles. On him, it is adorable.

At dinner, I say to my husband, "I think it is time for a change." My thirteen-year-old daughter, Kayla, snorts.

"What kind of change?" Jerry asks.

"A real one this time," I answer. "I think I'm going to get a Fitbit."

"What is that?" Kayla asks as Ryder slaps a hand on the tray of his high chair.

"It's like a watch that tells you how active you are."

"Why do you need a watch to tell you how active you are?" Jerry asks.

"It'll keep me motivated," I say and scoop another bite of orchard-fruit medley into Ryder's waiting mouth.

"It's a lot of money to spend on something we don't really need," he says. Kayla has pulled her phone out and is texting her friends. The television blares as the news comes on.

"Don't undermine my success, Jerry," I say.

Kohl's choice to name the color of the room *Lemon Twist* is one of those details that sets the tone for the piece. The main character tries to be bright and cheery like that color, but she's disappointed by her *plump belly* and *cankles*—sweeter versions of other descriptors. Especially evident here is the writer's attitude toward her subject. Rather than mopingabout body issues, this is a story about fighting for self-worth, summed up perfectly in the line delivered at the end of this excerpt: *"Don't undermine my success, Jerry."*

Last, we have a story from writer Bree Barton, who is a master of syntax.

(excerpt from) **SEXING THE STARLING**
by Bree Barton
Published in *Mid-American Review*, July 2016

My name is Sunshine. They say it's a fat girl's name, but I'm only a little bit fat. I was named for the shaft of light that slipped through the bathroom window and fell on the $9.99 pregnancy test my mother bought at the drugstore. The way she tells the story, it was the middle of July and it wouldn't stop raining. The rain made her horny, which is why she fucked sixteen men that summer, which is why I have no idea who my father is.

"You were the sunbeam," she says, "in the warm summer rain."

I like that expression, *warm summer rain*, because I can bisect each word down the middle, hang it over a little hook in my mind.

Bend it into two equal halves between *wa* and *rm*, *sum* and *mer*, *ra* and *in*. I spend a lot of time bisecting words. I feel conflicted about some words, especially *mom* and *dad*, because *mom* would hang oh-so-perfectly over the hook, but I'd have to hang it on the *o* and I don't like disturbing the letters themselves. I much prefer hanging words in the sliver of a spacebetween.

"You should get her into crafts," Stone's mother tells my mother. Stone is my best friend in the eighth grade. "She'd be great at crafts. Such a busy little mind."

So my mother finds a "Taxidermy for Teens!" class and signs me up. She waits to tell me until after dinner when I am poring over her magazine, the one with nude male models on each glossy page.

"I don't want to skin a dead bird, Mom."

Barton's artful syntax begins in the third paragraph. She allows her character to literally play with words on the page, breaking them apart and fitting them back together, ending in a made-up word, *spacebetween*. The juxtaposition of this wordplay and the nearly monotone dialogue adds up to a fresh, original voice.

Each of these stories has a strong identifiable style. The writer's voice shines through, right from the opening words. The next time you read a short story or an essay, see if you can pick out examples of diction, detail, imagery, syntax, and tone. Then look at your own writing. What do you see?

TEN TIPS FOR STRENGTHENING YOUR VOICE

You'll know you have a distinct voice when somebody says to you, "I would know your work anywhere." Usually it's a mentor or critique partner who says this to you first; later, you'll hear it from readers. Honing your voice is important, but how do you make your current writing shine brighter? Try these ten tips:

1. Expand your vocabulary. Read widely, study your thesaurus, and buy one of those "word of the day" calendars.

2. Study sentence structure. Do you miss sentence diagraming? Me too! Go old school, and play with words again. Subject-verb-object, oh my!

3. Give grammar another look. Even the most competent writer can benefit from brushing up on her grammar skills. Knowing the rules of grammar increases your confidence when you write—and saves you time in the editing stage.

4. Magnify the details. Be specific and intimate in your descriptions of the people, settings, and actions on the page. Every word in dialogue, action, interiority, and narration counts. Choose your words with purpose.

5. Get sensual. Make a list of sensory words for each of the five senses, and challenge yourself to use them. Add at least two to every essay or story you write.

6. Take risks. Let your instincts guide your decisions. That word choice that you think might be a little too strange? Try it. You might love it. It might become your signature one of these days.

7. Practice your hooks. Great essays and short stories begin with terrific first lines. What words could you choose to make that happen?

8. Practice exits. Leave your readers with one last resonant line. Or even one great word. Plan to make every short story and essay memorable.

9. Create lists. Make a list of things you care about, and then write about those things. They will become the themes in your writing life.

10. Read, read, read. Reading is a great way to examine other writers' choices. Study what makes their voice unique, and then experiment on your own pages.

To put it simply, strengthening your writing skills will strengthen your voice. The longer you write, the more developed your voice will become.

VOICE EXERCISE: AMPLIFY THE DETAILS

Practicing originality in your details and descriptions is a great way to discover your organic voice. When you push yourself to think beyond your first or second idea, you allow yourself to dig deep, to find the root of your voice. The following exercise is intended to get you thinking about interesting ways to describe people, places, and objects. Your task is to let go of any expectations. Think beyond the obvious. Allow any words to come to you during the exercise—the more unusual, the better.

1. Write this list of nouns across the top of a piece of paper: *AUTO, PERSON, SKY, TREE*. Under each item, add three visual descriptors (can be phrases or words). For example: *AUTO: Ferrari, yellow, black scrape shaped like a penguin*

2. Add three audio descriptors to each noun. Example: *AUTO: engine reminds me of a metronome, revving like a hungry linebacker, exhausted ping of the cooling engine*

3. Now add three scents to your list. Example: *AUTO: the perfume of leather seats, musty cigarette ash, smoked tire treads*

4. Think of ways to describe what each noun might feel like. Add them to your columns. Example: *AUTO: rough rusty dents, crusty dry carpet, worn leather seats*

5. Circle three of your most unique answers for each noun. Write a short paragraph that uses all three descriptors.

I've performed part of this exercise to give you an example:

AUTO	PERSON	SKY	TREE
primer gray	blue-green eyes	passenger airplane	curling white bark
older than my grandfather	a mole on the side of the nose	uninterrupted blue sheet	orange leaves
one red door	white pantsuit	one star in the darkness	branches too long for its body
puttering engine	humming broadway tunes	airplane engine roars	wind whistling through leaves
screeching brakes	smoker-lung coughs	geese honk as they v-fly by	cracking of wood in a storm
the scrape of dry wiper on glass	clears throat at beginning of sentences	bee buzzes overhead	the screaming of an angry morning bird
burning oil	heavy Old Spice cologne	desert creosote	rotting fruit

molding seat stuffing	smoke on the breath	smoke from distant fireplace	pine
engine smoke	a fresh carnation in the lapel	saltwater mist	cedar
rough to the touch	damp hair	damp	rough trunk
tough leather on aging seats	rough chin	nose-drying lack of humidity	satin leaves
crusty carpet	silky fabrics	biting cold on my neck	supportive branches to sit on

Writing & Selling Short Stories & Personal Essays

4

SCENE WRITING

Now that you're thinking about your personal writing style, let's talk about how to showcase that style: the scene. Scenes are the building blocks of short stories and essays. They are the self-contained passages within your prose where you *show* instead of *tell*.

A scene is *action*.

The reader is sitting nearby, taking it all in. You are, as a writer, "showing" the action through stage direction and dialogue. To put it simply, a scene is where something actually happens: A pen drops; a siren wails in the distance; a mother shushes her baby; people flirt, fight, and buy ice cream.

The alternative to writing a scene is to write a passage of narration. Narration refers to those places where you "tell" your reader some things: the time of day, the setting, what someone is thinking. Transitions between scenes are often narrative passages; some openings are, too. Narration compresses information that you need to convey, but it isn't nearly as engaging as a scene. Save narration for places in your prose that don't require action—such as transitions.

Scenes make the reading experience feel real. They focus reader attention on the physical world and actions of the story. It's your job—through scene writing—to make readers feel like they are in the same room as your characters.

The scene has one more caveat: A scene is where something happens that changes the story. Your story has to keep moving forward. Tension must escalate. A strong scene will ensure that.

ELEMENTS OF A COMPELLING SCENE

Every scene needs to accomplish the task of moving your story or essay along in an interesting way. This is accomplished by the elements of *event, function, structure,* and *pulse*. Use each of these elements purposefully in your prose:

1. **EVENT:** Identify the occasion you're going to write about. Why are these characters or people in this space together? Is it a chance meeting on the street? A party? A morning in the kitchen?
2. **FUNCTION:** How is this scene going to advance your story or essay? Will this scene reveal new information? Showcase a confrontation? Pose a question? Reveal a decision? Create a pause for reflection? Sometimes your entire story or essay will take place in one scene. What then is the function of the "fly on the wall" moments you show?
3. **STRUCTURE:** Every scene needs a beginning, middle, and end. You begin with your main character's short-term goal (finding his car keys, persuading her teacher to change a grade, firing the gardener, etc.). From there, your scene is a volley of action and reaction, concluding with the accomplishment or failure to achieve the goal. Either way, by the end of the scene, there is a change, which will lead to the next event in your story.
4. **PULSE:** Pulse is the thumping heart beneath the prose—what makes this scene matter to the reader. It's what gives the scene momentum: emotion, desire, need, motivation.

"To me, a scene is the basic measuring unit by which we construct our pieces. When these units are identified, they immediately become distinct. They are then mobile and flexible. They can

be seen as weak or strong. They can be put in a different order, creating a very different result."

—STUART HORWITZ

....

My short story, "What Happens Next," takes place all in one scene. Very short stories often do. Here, I've noted the four elements discussed in this section: event, function, structure, and pulse.

WHAT HAPPENS NEXT
Published in *The Sunlight Press*, January 2017
by Windy Lynn Harris

His eyes search me for help while the nurse urges him to sit up. He doesn't want to do this, but I can't will myself to defy the medical authority in the room. I don't know what to say.

I'm not in charge here.

He's supposed to get moving now, though they've only stitched him up a day back. [*The event is revealed: This man is recovering from surgery.*] It was the kind of tumor you can recover from, though the surgery itself was long and dangerous. Monitors beep and pulse in the room. I haven't brushed my teeth yet. A whooshing sound announces an automatic blood-pressure check. If this was a television show, they'd let him rest.

The nurse sets a walker near his bed, and I know already that it isn't big enough for him. He's far too tall for the little chrome contraption at his side, but I don't say anything. Instead, I watch the nurse adjust the handles. [*The function of the "fly on the wall" moments are to show the narrator's struggle to understand her role in this situation.*] She purses her mouth while my husband pulls his long tired legs from under the covers. It's too short, of course. It's far too short.

She tells him they might have a different walker, and then she tells me she'll be back.

When she's gone, I come to his side. I almost sit down on the bed next to him, but he shakes his head, lifts a tube. There are many things plugged into him, around him. He doesn't want to do this, and I'm a betrayer.

The nurse returns with a man in scrubs. He has a wide smile and a walker made for athletes. He's got jokes and quick hands. Soon, my husband is up. He's bent too far forward, but he doesn't straighten. His grip is white on the handles.

The male nurse adjusts the tubes and bags and the long white cord attached to my husband's finger.

I hold the door open and watch my husband take shaky steps toward me. [*The structure looks like this: The narrator's goal is to help her husband. The action and reaction moments happen as the nurse tries to get him out of bed and to the door. The walker is too short. A second nurse comes to help. The husband does make it to the door by the end of the scene, with the narrator finally finding a small way to help: by holding the door.*] A gurney passes the doorway, rolling another woman's husband to his room. He's fresh from the intensive-care unit. I know this because his wife is trailing behind with his overnight bag and she's having trouble keeping up.

Over the next six weeks, I'll become an expert in breathing exercises and pancreatic-fluid calculations. I'll meet a seventy-five-year-old poet named Joan, and I'll crush a huge black spider in the women's-bathroom sink. I'll cry in the parking garage twice, and on one of those days, I'll finally call my father and then I'll regret calling my father and I will seriously think about buying a pack of cigarettes but I will be too tired to stop at a store.

My husband nears me at the door, and I don't understand the look on his face. [*The pulse is heard throughout this story in the narrator's interiority. She is sad and disappointed that she can't do anything more significant to help her husband.*] I smile at him and wait for him to smile back. He looks down at the scuffed linoleum as he shuffle-walks past me. I close the door behind us. He's supposed to go all the way to the nurse's station on this first journey, and I'm supposed to cheer him on. I'm supposed to be the one who knows what happens next.

Scene Openings

You don't have much space when writing short stories and essays, so each scene should have a reason for inclusion. Short works tend to have only a few scenes, and some may only contain one. Make the most of this terrific storytelling tool by starting off strong.

Writing & Selling Short Stories & Personal Essays

Begin your scene at an interesting moment for your readers. Don't start with the weather—that's narrative. The actual scene begins when you zoom in on the action. Make that action something worthy of the space you've given it. Show someone in conflict. Don't bother showing a woman driving to a party unless that drive is something interesting to watch and meaningful to your overall story. Instead, begin your scene at the moment that the party's hostess greets this woman at the door and pretends not to know her.

Always orient your reader to the current time and place. Give subtle clues if you'd like, but there isn't anything wrong with saying, "I arrived at my mother's funeral to find two angry brothers and a sobbing priest."

Just as important, your readers need to know *when* this scene is happening. If this is a piece about your childhood, let readers know your age or how long ago this event took place. If it is a futuristic science-fiction story, make sure readers understand that this isn't taking place today.

If this is the second scene of a story or essay, make sure readers know how much time has passed between scenes. Consider something simple like this: "The next morning, I found Richard wading through our mother's courtyard fountain with his pants rolled up, plucking out coins."

Action and Reaction

Every scene is a volley between action and reaction. An event happens, causing a character to respond. This pattern isn't something you need to learn from scratch—you already know it. It's the pattern of basic human participation.

For example, say you're writing about the time you wanted a promotion (or you're writing a short story about someone who wants a promotion). To start, you ask your boss for a promotion. Your boss doesn't think you're ready, so he says, "No." You really want the job, so you articulate your qualifications. You're told the position has already been assigned to your assistant. You slam your fist on the desk and demand to talk to management. You're told to get out of the office. You reach for a stapler and aim it at your boss's head. And so on. Every action had a reaction, and that reaction was an action worthy of its own reaction.

Each reaction moment is actually a complex internal process. First, we have an emotion. Next, we have a thought. These two items might sound too similar to bother separating, but both have their own function. Emotion is organic, and that emotion spurs a thought. That thought is the moment we assess the situation. Both of these reaction beats are important when telling your stories. They help illuminate character motivation.

We can highlight the reaction beats in our example by zooming in closer. Let's look back at the moment you asked your boss for a raise. He said, "No." Your first response isn't the line of dialogue where you express your qualifications. Your first response was an emotion. Maybe you felt annoyed, shocked, or angry. Any emotion can then spur a thought. That thought might be: *I can't believe he's going to make me beg.* It could also be: *He knows I was the one to save the Adams account.* Whatever the thought is, that's the moment when you (or your character) are assessing the situation and preparing an appropriate reaction.

Tip: The intricacies of your essay or story's reaction moments might be tougher to spot than action moments, and that's a good thing. Reactions should be subtle. We have an emotion and then a thought, but there might only be a second or two between these things and they don't each require a spotlight in your prose, especially during emotionally charged moments.

In a scene, this volley of action and reaction happens constantly, but there is also an overall scene pattern: goal, conflict, disaster, emotion, thought, decision, action. Those first three items identify scene-specific action moments, and the last four are bigger-picture reaction moments. Let's take a closer look at each of them here:

Action Beats

GOAL: What does the character or narrator want in this scene? In our example, the goal is to get a promotion.

CONFLICT: Why can't that character have it right now? The boss said "no" and continues to say "no" in an action-and-reaction pattern that leads to the disaster.

DISASTER: This is an obvious obstacle, the unanticipated but logical moment that relates to the goal. It's the moment your narrative turns. Disaster can come early or late in the scene. Without it, the scene is boring. In our example, this is the moment when your boss tells you that your assistant has already been given the job you want.

Reaction Beats

EMOTION: As humans, our first response is almost always an emotion. Your stories and essays need to reflect that. In our example, that emotion is anger (shown by your slamming your fist on the desk).

THOUGHT: We process our reaction by labeling our feelings. We process in this order: review, analyze, plan. In our example, you demand to speak to management—this is how you review your circumstances, analyze your worth. You plan to plead your case, but wait; your boss wants you out of the office.

DECISION: We decide what we should do next. This can be rational or irrational, and in this case, it's irrational.

ACTION: We take the first step toward our plan. You pick up the stapler.

....

"Small motions give a static scene energy. This is especially true for scenes that are dialogue-heavy. When something is moving around in the background or off to the side of the central event/conversation, that motion makes the reader more aware of the stakes."

—JEANNE LYET GASSMAN

....

A Look at Conflict in Scenes

Characters have personal agendas that drive their decisions and actions. Secondary characters have goals, too, and sometimes those goals are in direct opposition to the goals of the main character. This causes fantastic, story-worthy conflict.

Tension and conflict will keep your readers turning the page. Raise the emotional stakes in your conflict whenever you can. Emotional stakes include suffering, sacrifice, jeopardy, sexual tension, and frustration, among others. You can use venting, praying, whining, and cajoling to reveal the emotional stakes. Ask yourself, "Where can I include one or more of these in my current piece of work?"

Not all conflict is as direct as two people battling it out, though. Conflict worth reading about can also be caused by poor health, dangerous weather, low self-esteem, and other less-obvious problems. Anytime a person's goal hits a hurdle, you've got conflict. Your job is to add tension through acceleration, which increases reader involvement. Make your readers wonder: *Will he ever walk again? Will she be brave enough to tell her mother the truth? Will she reach the phone in time to hear his last words?*

How to End a Scene

You'll want to end a scene when the tension is released. That doesn't mean a moment when the conflict has been resolved, but it could. Maybe it's a moment when someone has made a declaration or an offer. A time when there has been an interruption. An agreement. A kiss. It can be a moment, especially when writing essays, where you want to pause for personal reflection.

Think about the last thing you want to give readers in your scene. What do you want them to feel? Do you want them to worry? Empathize? Cry? You, the writer, have some say in that. Choose words purposefully to convey the emotion you want readers to experience.

This moment doesn't require much wrap-up, if any. Show that interruption or agreement or kiss, and end the scene right there. No need to explain anything further or translate the events in some concessionary sentence. Just move ahead to the next scene. Your readers will interpret the events for themselves.

Make Every Scene Count

1. **OPEN YOUR SCENE AT THE LAST POSSIBLE MOMENT.** No need to give any backstory. Jump right into an important moment. Your scenes are jewels on a necklace with gold narrative holding them together. Each scene must be worthy of its place on that necklace, a gleaming well-cut gem.
2. **ALWAYS END YOUR SCENES BY RELEASING TENSION.** Don't summarize for your readers. Get out, and move on.
3. **CHOOSE THE RIGHT POINT-OF-VIEW CHARACTER FOR THE SCENE.** In any essay, you—the writer—are going to be the main character, but sometimes you might tell a story through someone else's eyes. It's these times when you'll have a choice. In any scene, your main character should be the person with the most to lose. They are the most interesting to watch because they have something at stake. Their goal feels the most compelling.
4. **HAVE A CLEAR IDEA OF WHY EACH SCENE IS INCLUDED IN YOUR PROSE.** Ask yourself, *Why is this moment a scene instead of a summary? What about this scene furthers the overall narrative of my piece?* If you have a difficult time answering these questions, you need to rethink your choice. Perhaps you need to compress the scene into a summary instead.

TEN QUESTIONS FOR TIGHTENING YOUR SCENES

Every scene in your essay or short story deserves your focused attention. At the revision stage, consider the following ten questions for each of your scenes:

1. Is the time frame obvious to readers?
2. Did you begin the scene when something important happens?

3. Does the dialogue advance the plot, reveal character, and heighten tension?
4. Did something significant happen?
5. Was this relevant to the conflict?
6. Is the main character's or narrator's goal clear?
7. Does the scene have tension, and does that tension build?
8. Does the scene end when the tension is released?
9. Are your actions and reactions balanced?
10. Is there a shift in the overall story because of this scene? Discovery, revelation, recognition?

SCENE EXERCISE: WHO/WHAT/WHY

This is a great exercise for practicing action and reaction beats in your story: First, think of two people. They can be lovers or co-workers, neighbors or family members. Any two will do. Write their names side by side on a piece of paper.

Next, answer these three questions about both people, and fill in your answers in their respective columns:

1. Who is this person?
2. What do they want today?
3. Why is this want important?

Examine the motivations of these two people. They each have a personal agenda. Those agendas might be similar, but maybe their consequences are different. Maybe someone risks losing love, while the other person only risks missing a movie.

But what if they were in the same scene together and in conflict for some reason? How would they engage? Would they be confrontational? Complementary? Or would they ignore each other completely? Write that scene.

I've performed this exercise myself to give you an example:

MARGARET	RICHARD
Margaret is Richard's tenant and upstairs neighbor. She lives alone with a cat she isn't supposed to have.	Richard owns the building that he and Margaret (and two other families) call home.
Margaret wants Richard to replace the apartment's small white refrigerator that stopped working that morning—without him learning about her cat.	Richard owes an amount in gambling debt that he can't seem to surmount. He hasn't been on top for years. He wants to fix the fridge upstairs rather than replace it, but he doesn't want Margaret to think he's cheap. She's got the other families in the building talking about repairs already, and it could get out of hand.
Margaret is hiding from her abusive husband. If she gets evicted from her apartment, she'll have to reach out to family for help, and that could lead to her husband finding her.	If the lady upstairs gets pushy about replacing the thing, he'll have to find a way to quiet her down before everyone wants a new fridge.

5

SETTING

Setting refers to the *when* and *where* of a short story or essay. It's the place and time in which your characters are acting. But setting isn't just backdrop. Setting can influence theme, characters, and action. Choose your setting purposefully, from the first paragraph to the last.

Essays and short stories usually take place in only one or two locations, but the number could vary. Each environment you show can illuminate your overall story. To cut down on verbosity, be specific when you describe your settings. Use concrete nouns with distinctive connotations that allow the reader to fill in some of the details for you. Instead of writing *building*, you can write *skyscraper, dormitory*, or *courthouse* instead.

Another way to economize is to show the time of day, the climate, the weather, or the landscape, with the intention of conveying emotion. A stormy day can mirror sorrow. A vast desert can echo a theme about being lost in the world. A broken clock can remind readers that the character doesn't have much time left to figure out his dilemma.

Lisa Fugard is a novelist who also writes short stories and personal essays. She's a terrific writing instructor, too—my partner in the creation of Storytelling Boot Camp. Here's what Lisa has to say about setting"

> Working with setting is not about describing the beach or the restaurant or the mountain slope in the first paragraph and then letting all

sense of place fall away. Do so and you risk losing your readers. Instead, it's about carefully selecting specific sensory details to maintain the sense of place, to set the atmosphere, to reveal character, to foreshadow and amplify the theme of your story or essay. You are searching for the detail that opens up the narrative universe for your readers, not one that has them admiring your beautiful prose—tempting as that may be. One specific detail carries far more power than ten generalities. You want the detail that leads your readers deeper and deeper into your story and activates their imaginations—the detail that has them turning the page because they are invested in your characters.

CONTINUE TO REVEAL SETTING THROUGHOUT YOUR PROSE

Begin your exploration of setting by thinking about the broader environment you intend to show readers, along with the things that are right at hand. What does this place look like? Is it a crowded pizza parlor or a church on Tuesday morning? What can you hear? Birds? Dripping water? A nearby train? What is the weather like? Tropical? Breezy? Snowy? Damp? What is she holding? Do you see a flag? Use the details you've chosen to establish an opening mood or tone for your piece. For example, if you're writing an essay about a time when you felt hopeless, zero in on the bleakest details available—the gray carpet or the rain-soaked jacket in a heap at your feet, perhaps. Darken the lighting.

During your story, think about a central unifying aspect of your setting that you can repeatedly show for maximum effect. Maybe the weather changes as the story unfolds, or you keep coming back to the veins on the back of your mother's hand. Maybe it's the smell of strawberries that you weave through the piece.

Every character will react to an environment differently. For instance, some people like rain and some don't. Showing reactions to an environment can reveal new information about your character (or yourself). When you allow your characters to interact with the environment, you can create stronger emotion and conflict. For example, if you want to reveal how uncomfortable your Uncle Harry is when he's in a crowd, study his physical stance under this stress. Zoom in on his feet. Is he fidgety? Does he roll his ankle around like he's warming up for a sprint? Or does he plant his feet far apart, establishing a safe zone for himself?

Think about putting your characters in unexpected settings. The environment in your plot can add layers to your story. For example, if you're writing fiction, maybe you chose to have two people argue about doing the dishes while they're seated in the balcony at an opera or in the upper deck of a baseball game. When writing an essay, why not reflect on the bad news from the doctor somewhere other than the doctor's office? How about a busy playground? An airport?

Sensory Details

Specific details make a setting come alive, but there's no need to be wordy. A few well-placed sensory details can save you space on the page while introducing a setting that readers can see and feel. For example: "When we'd passed the outlet mall and the casino, the I-10 became a lonelier road. It narrowed into two skinny lanes. As expected, the haulers took over the right, their fat cargo nearly riding the white dotted line that separated us."

Consider all five senses when you show the places that matter to your story. Let the reader see, hear, smell, taste, and touch the things you describe around them. Every environment has a source of light, a scent, landmarks or symbols, sounds, etc. And all of these things can create a specific mood for your scene's backdrop.

TEN TIPS TO WRITING A MEMORABLE SETTING

There's nothing very interesting about watching two people on a date in a nice restaurant. But if the restaurant is decaying, with peeling wallpaper and chipped dishes, then we start to feel a somber mood. Suppose a fly keeps buzzing around one of them, and maybe the restaurant smells like one of those tree-shaped car fresheners. That's a setting you'll remember. Here are ten tips to getting it right:

1. Your opening paragraph needs to settle readers into your piece. They'll be searching for the who/what/why of your essay or story. Use setting in your opening as a way to orient them. Give clues about the location or the year that your narrative takes place.

2. Don't use the generic version of anything—not a room, not a hospital, not a car. Always give your setting at least one interesting detail. Maybe the room has a carpet stain in the shape of a human skull. Perhaps the hospital is so close to the freeway that you can hear the rush of cars from the parking lot. Maybe the rental car your character is driving smells like a wet dog.

3. Think about the sources of light. Is it a foggy day at the beach? Are you in a room with tall windows? A supermarket aisle lit by fluorescent lights? These images create a background.

4. Think about sound. Is there an elementary school nearby, or is your story set on a desert island filled with exotic birds?

5. Don't use the first adjectives that come to mind. If you imagine a character's car to be a sexy red sports car, stop and ponder your choice. What if the car had zebra stripes instead? What would that say about your character? What if the car was bubblegum pink?

6. Find ways of matching your setting to the tone of your scene. Images have connotations, so use them to your advantage. If you're showing a tense argument between two people, perhaps you point out the storm brewing in the distance or the pot of chili on the stove that's about to boil over. For other situations, you might consider how vegetation and water can create feelings of cool refreshment. Fireplaces and candles remind of us romance. Shadows make us worry.

7. Settings can have a flavor, at times. Some settings taste like salty air. Some dry your mouth.

8. Think about scents. They evoke memories so quickly. Flowers, smoke, a cake baking in the oven, and gasoline are all vivid and universal scents that will remind your readers of moments from their own lives. Make your descriptions of universal scents unique to your story by showing your characters reacting to them.

9. Be consistent with your setting. If you mention a gathering of ducks on the front lawn as your character enters the house, revisit the setting when she leaves. Either the ducks are still there, or they've moved. Maybe they're gone for good. Your readers will want to know.

10. Use setting to enhance your ending. Sticking the last note is essential, and setting can help. Let the environment reflect the last mood you want to leave your readers with. When you want them to feel hope, brighten the lighting. Add rain to represent a cleansing. A strong wind can bring with it the feeling of change.

SETTING EXERCISE: CREATE A SENSORY-RESOURCE LIST

The settings we show in short stories and essays have to feel complete, and we only have so many words to use. Using specific sensory setting details can elevate your prose without taking up much space on the page. To make your job easier, create a bank of interesting setting words for anytime you feel stuck. I like to use a spiral notebook for this exercise because I can keep adding to it.

On one page, write the word *home* in the center of the paper and circle it. Next, fill every bit of space left on the page with better words to describe home. Anything that comes to you, write it down. Use all five senses somewhere in your collage of words.

Next, write the word *work* on a different piece of paper. Circle the word *work*, and fill in the rest of the page with specific sensory details about *work*, remembering to use each of the five senses at least once. Continue your bank of sensory setting adjectives by using these words in the center of other pages: *storm, childhood, vacation, school, commute,* and *gym.*

Revisit these pages whenever you feel your setting needs better adjectives.

I've performed this exercise myself as an example:

HOME

bungalow	quiet	adobe
rustic	rose-trellised	retirement
Victorian	condo	town house
contemporary	cottage	tenement
suburban	beloved	apartment
stately	spacious	
remodeled	duplex	

CHARACTERS

Delivering full-formed characters can be difficult when writing short stories and personal essays. You don't have the ability to develop deep characterization when you only have a few pages to work within, yet you need to make a character shine just as much as he would if you were writing a 400-page novel. The key to success is to let characterization work double-duty. Reveal your characters through action, speech, appearance, and thought. Blend these elements together to amplify characterization while writing economically.

The people in our stories have the enormous task of delivering our plot and our themes through action and speech. Each one of them has desires, fears, hopes, and disappointments. You are in charge of how much page time each character gets and which ones are most important to your story. Be selective and purposeful with your characters. Each one must matter.

Every character—including an essay's narrator—has layers. Characters and people have a side they show the world and a side they only show to certain people. And then there's an inner self that's personal and private—the person with biases and judgments. Your goal as a writer is to reveal several layers in short prose so that a character's actions feel authentic.

CHANGE

During the course of your story or essay, a character must change. There must be a noticeable difference between his introduction and the conclusion. Every character must also be affected by the events you present. Even in a very short piece of writing, we want to know that the character we're following is capable of change.

In essay writing, showing vulnerability is key. It says to the reader, *I want things to be different than they are. I'm willing to examine myself closely, and therefore, I'm willing to change.*

In fiction, all readers need to see a tiny nugget that lets them see the main character caring deeply about something. This is all about showing empathy. Let your readers know that your main character has a goal worthy of achieving, and they'll root for her, even if she gets in her own way.

REAL PEOPLE IN YOUR STORIES ARE CHARACTERS, TOO

You need to know your characters intimately to write about them authentically. This is especially important to remember when you're writing essays. Your audience doesn't know the people in your life. They don't know anything that you don't tell them.

When writing true stories, take the time to *study* the people you're including. Show your audience specific details about them that reveal their respective inner dispositions and motivations. Take a step back, and allow yourself to see this person as a participant in your narrative. Why does she belong there? What do readers need to better understand about them as characters in your narrative? As a writer, your goal is to take real-life people and rebuild them as characters. That involves reconstructing them for readers who have never met them before.

Character Development for Short Prose

Character study can be divided into three categories:

1. Physical (appearance, age, gender, etc.)
2. Social (occupation, family, politics, religion)
3. Personality (habits, ambitions, secrets, hobbies)

Character-development worksheets are easy to find online with a quick Google search. These studies are basically a comprehensive character sketch that includes items from all three of the character-study categories. A worksheet will include everything you need to know about each character in your story, such as "eye color," "worst habit," "greatest fear," "ultimate vacation spot," etc.

Even though most of the information included in a character-development worksheet won't make it into your story, these development tools are perfect for characters in novels and memoir projects because they become a reference guide for the author. The worksheet is a snapshot of an overall picture, even if the narrative is only a few years of that person's life.

But what about short-story and essay writing? Do we really need to know that much about the characters in short prose? The answer is, simply, no. Short prose is intimate, immediate, and specific to the event you're focused on in your story. You don't have room for much backstory (if any), and you can't rely on long passages of narration. From your first sentence, each detail you reveal about your character has to illuminate something about her.

You can create a character that feels complete by revealing four very basic things your readers need to know: *name, trait, desire, hurdle*. This list is short but incredibly important. Let's take a closer look at each one.

Name

When writing an essay, you have real people and their actual names to work with—but that doesn't mean you can't be creative. Perhaps you can use a nickname or reveal something about yourself as a narrator by creating a nickname during narrative reflection—"Uncle Whisky Breath" or "Perfect Little Sarah," for example. Someone you refer to as "Little Rick," instead of just "Rick," can give readers a sense of how you see yourself in relation to this person. This characterizes you, as the narrator.

When writing fiction, be purposeful in your choice of names. Your character's name should convey some aspect of her identity. Choose a name that fits the part of the country this person is from, the mood of the story, or even the time of the setting. Names like "Gertrude" and "Howard" feel slightly out of fashion and therefore bring an older person to mind. "Chet" and "Buffy" probably make you think of matching v-neck sweaters. The name "Alexandra" has a completely different connotation to your readers than the name "Kitty." And what about this line: *Fat Nose Jim eyed me like a juicy steak.* Readers don't need more than this to clearly visualize Jim. Maybe there are slightly different versions of Jim in each reader's head, but they all see a big guy, tough, not too handsome. And all that just because you named him *Fat Nose Jim.*

Personal Trait

Want to create a memorable character? Highlight his most unusual personal trait. Maybe he has scabs on his hands that won't heal, or he has white-blonde hair unlike any you've ever seen. Perhaps he plays the violin left-handed or clicks his teeth together when he's excited. Maybe he only smiles with half of his face, or he smells like lavender, even on the ball field after a long game.

In essay writing, the writer is the narrator of a true story, which makes it difficult to remember to look at yourself. Take a moment for inventory. What are the most memorable things about you? They can be physical traits or social tics. Do you have a wandering eye, making it difficult for people to maintain a conversation with you? Do you play air drums while you drive? Do you sweat during tense moments or conflicts? Do you forget people's names? Do you have a strong handshake? Do people always say they love your accent?

When you're writing fiction, try to find the most unique character trait to highlight, and then match it to a personality. Example: Give a shy woman the prominent trait of looking up to the sky when someone is talking to her. Normally, shy people avoid eye contact, so this feels authentic, but the added detail is unusual enough for your readers to remember. They'll know she's shy, but they'll also be wondering why she looks up. And you, the writer, get to decide the reason, adding another layer to your story. Perhaps she's religious or thinks there are messages waiting for her in the clouds. The reasoning can appear in your story once you've provided the unusual detail.

Desire

We talked about character goals in the scene section, and we need to talk about goals again here. Your characters, whether fictional or real, all want something. A character's desire is the reason for his actions. In short prose, readers need to see the people as believable, and one way to show authenticity is to reveal their ambitions. Characters—like people—have wants and desires.

What the heck do your characters really want, though? What do they want in the short term, and what do they want in their hearts? Are they hiding a secret? Trying to persuade someone? Seduce someone? Get out of a speeding ticket?

Say you're writing an essay about the time that you went to the movies with your father and his car was stolen from the parking lot. When you got out to the parking lot with your father, you might have been shocked by your father's words. Maybe he was fine but swore because the thief ruined your after-movie plans. Any and every detail should be driven by some deep need. Maybe your need to feel secure was shattered, or maybe you needed a shopping trip with your father for a specific purpose. Either one works. For added effect, consider showing opposing desires.

Hurdle

What is keeping your main character from her goals? There are physical hurdles (ex: age, money, other people, a disability) and emotional ones (ex: a breakup, the loss of a pet). Maybe she tries to talk to someone, and he ignores her. Maybe your character wants to go hiking but sees a diamondback snake at the trailhead. Maybe she is on a plane that has just run out of fuel. All of these hurdles can be compelling, but hurdles that she puts in front of herself can reveal character. Self-sabotage tells us volumes about the saboteur. For example: A character who drinks too much the night before an important meeting is setting herself up for a consequence. Maybe she hates her job and wants to be fired so that she can restart her music career, or maybe she wants to prove to herself that she's still young enough to keep up an all-night pace the way she did when she was as young as the latest crop of new hires.

....

"Where do you find characters? Everywhere! They show up in newspaper stories, at the supermarket, from a snippet in an overheard conversation. Often they arise out of intriguing alchemical combinations. It's when you take the way your grandma so delicately slipped on her white gloves, wriggling her fingers like small white worms to get them to fit just so, and your lingering regret about not going to drama school and pour [all] this into a 72-year-old woman who enrolls in a three-day introductory course for magicians in Las Vegas. Give her an unmet need or a fear that governs her life, and there you have it—a character who will inevitably lead you into a story."

—LISA FUGARD
....

TEN TIPS FOR CREATING A FULLY-FORMED CHARACTER

1. Reveal the physical traits of your character—gender, age, and body type—and then zero in on the most interesting detail. Maybe he has

gray eyes that remind you of a wolf. Perhaps he has an old-fashioned handlebar mustache or a scar across his nose.

2. Every person has a history. If she grew up in a town with an unusual name, say so. If she grew up in poverty or great wealth, mention that, too. Details add to the reader's overall impression of this person.

3. Think about this person's family. Is she an only child? One of seven? Does she still talk to her parents? These details shape a person's attitude toward others.

4. What is this person's occupation, and how does he feel about it? Is he living his dream job, or does he wish he'd traveled another path in life?

5. Religion matters in your characterization if it matters to your story. If you're going to point out that the woman at the doctor's office is wearing a cross, you'll also need to let your readers know how you feel about that. Present your main character's own religious attitude as she observes this woman.

6. Politics, like religion, matters in your characterizations if it matters to your story. If you're going to designate someone as a Democrat or a Republican or anything else, you'll need to add an attitude toward that distinction.

7. Some people have habits that make them distinct. Think about your characters. Do they bite their nails, chew their lips, or twist their hair? If you're working with fictional people, consider taking these habits further. Maybe he bites his cuticles, scratches the corner of his mouth until it bleeds, or chews on the ends of his hair?

8. Think about who this person loves more than anyone else. Is it a spouse? A child? The woman across the street? Is their love mutual or one-sided?

9. Everyone has a big dream. What one thing does your character wish would happen in his life? Does he want to be rich or famous? Does he want to find his birth mother? Does he want to be vindicated for some wrong from the past?

10. Everyone has a secret. Your characters all have some seeds of hidden knowledge they keep close to their hearts. Maybe they keep it a secret so that someone else won't get hurt, or maybe they don't want to lose others' love and respect. Knowing your characters' biggest secrets can help you illuminate their motives.

CHARACTER EXERCISE: A BUBBLE MAP OF CHARACTER DETAILS

Thinking of a one-dimensional persona is easy: the doctor with poor handwriting, the muscle-bound fireman, the science teacher with thick glasses. Each of these stock characters has the potential to become an interesting lead, with some work. It's all a matter of closer examination.

For this exercise, you'll be creating a bubble map of interesting traits that one of these characters might have, traits that would pull him out of the ordinary and brand him as an original. First, write the word *doctor* or *fireman* or *teacher* in the middle of a page, and draw a circle around it. Then draw five spokes coming off of the circle. At the end of each spoke, give the character a new detail. For instance: fisherman, snappy dresser, eats mints all day, divorced, too thin.

Now circle each of those new details, and draw five more spokes. At the end of each spoke, write specific information about this trait. Maybe he is a world-class bass fisherman, or perhaps he still goes fishing with his father every year. He might be too thin because he's ill, but he could also be too thin because he's haunted by something his ex-wife said about his stomach. Write it all down. When you're done, select the most illuminating details to include in your work.

I've included an example of this exercise.

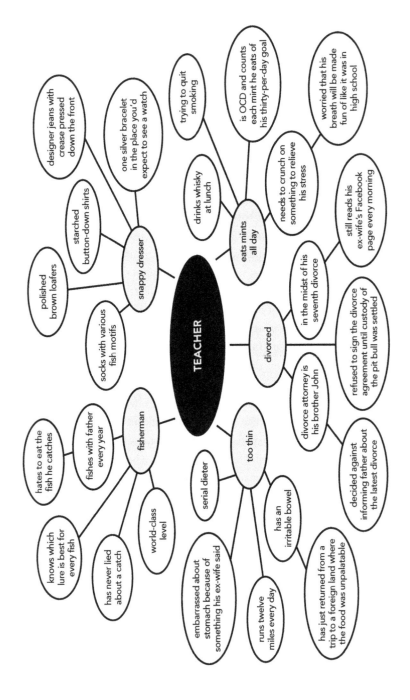

Writing & Selling Short Stories & Personal Essays

7

POINT OF VIEW

Choosing the right point of view is one of the most technical decisions you make as a writer, especially when writing short prose. POV determines whose eyes the reader experiences the story through (that person is called the viewpoint character). It's a key choice since different POVs can bring different elements to your prose. Pick a POV strategy that allows you to convey your theme in the shortest amount of space.

When writing an essay, you'll write in first-person POV, unless you decide to fictionalize your true story.

That's right; you have a choice of POV even when you're writing a true story.

How? Consider this: We've all had powerful, true moments of change happen in our lives. These authentic moments can be terrific material for a personal essay, but they can also be great inspiration for a short story.

But why would you ever want to fictionalize one of your true stories?

Because sometimes it's difficult to write about painful events. Fictionalizing your truth can give you a safe distance to explore what happened. Sometimes you might want to hide the fact that you're telling this true event because other people are involved; sometimes you want to hide the true event from people you know.

Whatever your reason, be assured that those moments you've actually lived through will bring authentic emotions to fictional prose, too.

When you want to take a true story from your life and retell it as fiction, all you need to do is rethink your POV choice.

AVAILABLE POV OPTIONS

The most common POVs in short stories and essays are first person and third person, but second-person storytelling is an option as well.

FIRST-PERSON POV: A story written in the first person is told with *I, me, mine* pronouns. This POV is effective in giving a sense of closeness to the character because readers experience the story directly through the narrator's eyes. With this type of storytelling, it can be easy to get the reader to identify and sympathize with your main character. It can feel as if the narrator is speaking directly to the reader, sharing something intimate and private.

Consider this: You have a story about a shy woman who travels to Bangladesh for the first time—alone. With first-person POV, you can place the reader in her head—seeing what she sees, feeling what she feels, smelling what she smells.

The main character in these stories can only witness scenes in which he is physically present, though, so you are limited to telling your story through this narrow perspective. If the main character doesn't know something, your reader can't either.

Example of first-person POV:

> The sun-warmed sand beneath my feet felt exotic and indulgent. It seemed impossible that seven days ago I was standing at a car dealership in Ohio watching my husband kiss Janice Letz.

SECOND-PERSON POV: Second person is told from the perspective of *you* and *your.* Think of an instruction manual telling you the steps you need to follow to finish a project. This POV is rare in storytelling because it is difficult to pull off successfully. Short stories and essays need to include a narrative arc, and this type of POV makes that tough to accomplish. Second-person storytelling is most often seen in experimental short pieces where the writer has intentionally mimicked an informational brochure in order to convey her story and theme.

Example of second-person POV:

> You should ask yourself a few questions before beginning this journey. For starters, why are you willing to travel to a dangerous region, and do you fully understand the consequences of your choice to leave America?

THIRD-PERSON POV: Third person is told from the perspective of a narrator who is not involved in the story. This is the most commonly used POV in fiction. All characters are referred to as *he* and *she* when writing in third person. Depending on the type of third-person POV you choose, your narrator might know the thoughts and feelings of all of your characters or only one of them.

Two common options for writing in third person are third-person limited and third-person omniscient. Let's take a closer look at these options.

- **THIRD-PERSON-LIMITED POV:** "Limited" means that the narrator only knows the thoughts and feelings of *one* character at a time. The advantage of using this POV is that it gives you a little more freedom to share information than you have in first-person POV, while still maintaining a tight focus. The reader gets to filter the events of the story through this one character's motivations and desires while hearing the narrator's voice. The caveat: Readers can only see the story through this one person's perspective. Here's an example of third-person-limited POV:

  > John pulled into his empty driveway and cut the engine. Lenora's car was gone, even though she'd just texted him a rant about how he was never home when she needed him. It had been like this for months, her picking fights that didn't make sense. John opened the briefcase on his passenger seat and pulled out the Henderson file. He looked up the number for Lenora's first husband.

- **THIRD-PERSON-OMNISCIENT POV:** In omniscient stories, the narrator knows all of the thoughts and opinions of every single character but maintains a God-like distance along the way. The narrator knows things that others don't and makes comments about what's happening during the scene. Here's an example of third-person-omniscient POV:

> Five days ago the three Clover brothers entered the Radcliffe building and paid the balance due to Federal Bank, which is how they came to own all thirty-two floors of downtown office space.

DISTANCE

Distance refers to how close the narrator is to the action, and it's something savvy writers navigate with purpose. Let's pretend that you have a motion-picture camera in your hands. You can zoom in and out anytime you'd like. You can show the most intimate detail on a woman's coat or show a flyover moment from a jet above the plains of Kansas.

You can adjust your focus exactly the same way in your prose. Zoom in close when you want intimacy. Show specific details. When you want to give the reader some distance, create a broader view and show the bigger environment.

Example:

> Monsoon rains pummeled the local mountain. A blond woman sat in her car near the entrance to the hiking trail. (*very distant*)

> Elizabeth Valentine looked at the mountain from the front seat of her car. She hated rain. (*closer*)

> Liz stubbed out her cigarette and cursed her ex-husband. He'd warned her about visiting Sedona during the monsoon season. Right again. The prick. (*closest*)

ONE MORE DECISION TO MAKE

Whichever point of view you decide to use, you'll also need to choose between past and present tense. Past tense is the most invisible and unobtrusive tense to write in, but present tense has an immediacy that can't be denied. The tense you choose should be the one that feels right for your story.

Example of past tense:

Before my mother's Saturday hair appointments, she dropped me off at Grammy's house. Grammy taught me how to play poker and bake pies during those long afternoons, and she gave me my first sip of gin.

Example of present tense:

My shoes squeak on the floor of Grammy's kitchen while we work. She hands me the rolling pin, and I hesitate before taking it. I'm not supposed to know more about baking than my mother, but I think I already do.

TEN TIPS TO GETTING THE MOST FROM YOUR POV

1. When using the first-person POV, many of your sentences will begin with *I*, but not all of them should. Find clever ways to reword things so that your page has a variety of sentence openings.
2. Make sure your viewpoint character has a voice readers enjoy. She'll be narrating the action, so let her personality shine through.
3. Your viewpoint character is the only eye readers can see your story through. You can't reveal any details that he doesn't know.
4. In any POV, you—the writer—should disappear into the background. Readers shouldn't notice you at all.
5. Keep your POV consistent throughout the story.
6. Consider the age and education of your viewpoint character, and select words and images appropriate for her vocabulary.
7. Narrators can be reliable or unreliable, depending on what you hope to achieve.
8. Narrators can give their opinions on things. In fact, they should.
9. Usually a narrator tells the story to "the reader," but sometimes the narrator addresses a specific person. That can give you an essay or story that feels like it's spoken rather then written, which can be a powerful way to convey your theme.
10. The POV you choose should be the one that will hold your readers' attention the best. You might need to experiment with your piece in a few different POVs before you hit the right note.

POV EXERCISE: FIRST-PERSON VS. THIRD-PERSON STORIES

A great way to practice the most common POVs—first person and third person—is to try them both with the same idea. In this exercise, you'll write a true story first and then rewrite it in third person.

First, choose a defining moment from your life—maybe your first kiss or your first day as a nursing intern. Anything that elicits an emotional response will do.

Write a two-page essay about this event, telling the absolute truth. Use first-person POV throughout the essay.

Next, take that same event and begin again. This time, use third-person POV. Use the pronouns *he, she,* and *them.* Let yourself wander away from the truth as you write the story. Give yourself a bit of emotional distance from the truth, too. Choose a different viewpoint. Let yourself write anything new that comes to you about this event. Maybe you will write a happier ending, or maybe you will change the lesson you learned. Perhaps you will let the whole thing happen in a completely different country. When you've finished your second piece, compare it to the first. Which version is more interesting to read? You've probably let yourself relax into one of these versions more than the other. Choose the one with the most risk on the page. That's the one you should revise for publication.

DIALOGUE

Writing strong passages of dialogue, whether we're telling true stories or crafting fiction, is an important skill to have as a writer. Dialogue moves plot forward, reveals information about your characters, and provides important story information. Because of its importance, you should never let your dialogue become mere fluff. Words between characters should always be more than a passing conversation.

When you're writing an essay, you have the authority to pick and choose which conversations you reveal to readers. You also have the authority to edit these conversations using the same dialogue techniques that you'd use in fiction, as long as the overall "truth" behind what was said still remains. This means that if you remember someone saying something hurtful to you but you don't remember exactly what he said, you can improvise or fabricate, as long as the dialogue still rings true to the event as you remember it.

But realistic dialogue in short stories and essays shouldn't equal real speech. Written dialogue is only the impression of our speech, not a direct match to the garbled way we actually speak to each other. Have you listened to a conversation lately? There are plenty of "ums" and "wells" and super-long breaths.

Make sure your characters speak their minds—clearly.

The best way to hear dialogue authentically is to read it aloud. Omit any chit-chat. You don't have time to have a character ask about the weather unless it matters to your story. No "How was your day?" either, unless you're layering in subtext or you're about to surprise your readers with the answer to that question.

....

"Weak dialogue undermines our narratives. In fiction, it can erode—sabotage even—a fine story. Dialogue should contribute and reveal character, and great dialogue serves the story. It is an element we can use to express conflict, tension, implication, subtext, microtension, and emotion. Used to sufficient effect, it is a tool to control pacing and contribute to momentum. Dialogue is a vital element of story, no matter the form of writing."

—APRIL BRADLEY

....

PASSAGES OF DIALOGUE CAN ELEVATE YOUR PROSE

Let's start with an example. Your main character, Amanda, wants to be invited to the dance by the cute older boy who works at the ice-cream parlor. You might have Amanda enter the ice-cream shop, spinning on her toes and humming his favorite song. When Jake, the boy, doesn't react to her hints, Amanda decides to try harder.

If you write the next part of the ice-cream shop scene without dialogue, it might look something like this:

> Jake barely listened to what Amanda had to say as he created an unstable two-scooped chocolate tower. It was obvious he was more interested in who'd be taking Lilly to the dance, just like every other boy at school.

This is an example of *telling*. Now, there isn't anything wrong with telling some of the scene like this, but it's not as compelling for what could be a significant scene. A summary paragraph *tells* the reader your story.

Passages of dialogue allow you to *show* the story instead. Consider the same scene with dialogue:

> Amanda leaned over the counter and watched Jake's forearm flex as he shaped her scoop of chocolate ice cream. "I heard there'll be two different bands on Saturday night for the dance," she said. "The first one's just a warm-up. They even ordered an ice sculpture."
>
> "Your sister Lilly's in my homeroom," Jake said. He didn't look up from his task. "Is she going to the dance with you, or does she have a date?" He forced the scoop onto her crisp sugar cone. Amanda heard something crack.
>
> "She'll probably have a date. It's that kind of thing, you know, formal. Everyone's pairing up."
>
> "Everyone?" Jake worked on her second scoop. He held the cone upright, mostly.
>
> "You know, for pictures and things," she said.
>
> Jake put the new scoop on top of the other one and tapped it down a little too rough. A small piece of sugar cone fell to the floor. "Lilly always orders strawberry when she comes in," he said.
>
> Amanda took the cone from Jake's outstretched hand. "She's into strawberry right now, but tomorrow she'll decide that something else is better. She gets bored. By next week it'll be chocolate chip, maybe even mint."
>
> Jake looked past her to the next customer. "Who is Lilly going with on Saturday?"
>
> "Who knows? Lilly has a whole list of guys who want to take her." Jake nodded but didn't ask more.
>
> "She made a chart to decide. Height, car, popularity rating, that kind of thing. She said she won't choose until Friday."
>
> Jake pointed to the cashier, who was waiting to take Amanda's money. "We sell a lot of mint chip," he said. "Tell Lilly I'll make sure we have it in stock."

The first example was intentionally boring to prove a point, but the difference between these two styles of revealing the same story is clear. In the second example, we are present and involved. We aren't *told* that Amanda is jealous of her sister; we're *shown* the jealousy, particularly when Amanda tells Jake about the dance-date chart. It's a more interesting way for the reader to learn information.

DIALOGUE TAGS

A "dialogue tag" (or attribution) is the phrase you put before or after the dialogue (*he said*, *she said*, *I replied*, etc.). Almost every time, *said* is the right choice. Readers barely notice it, and it keeps your pace going strong. Throw in an occasional *whispered* or *shouted* if you need to—or maybe some short stage direction—but don't get any fancier than that. It is easy to unnecessarily distract your readers with long or frilly attributions.

FORMATTING DIALOGUE

Dialogue should always:

- Begin on a new line for each new speaker
- Use double quotation marks around the words
- Have punctuation *inside* the quotation marks
- End with a comma if you're adding a dialogue tag or with a full stop if you're adding an action

For example:

> "Lucy, please step outside," the teacher said. "We need to talk."
> "What about?"
> "The lemon on my desk." She folded her arms.

Here's a closer look at dialogue punctuation and some specific situations:

1. When punctuating dialogue with commas and an attribution before the dialogue, the comma is placed after the attribution and the appropriate punctuation mark goes inside the quotation mark at the end of the dialogue:

> David said, "I was asked to leave the museum."

2. When punctuating dialogue with commas and adding an attribution after the dialogue, the comma is placed inside the quotation mark:

> "He walked me to my car," Linda said.

3. When you're punctuating dialogue with commas and adding a pronoun attribution, the comma is placed inside the quotation mark and the pronoun is not capitalized:

> "I love you," she said.

4. For a non-dialogue beat to break up a line of dialogue, use commas:

> "And then I realized," Jane said with a sigh, "that he'd lied to me."

10 TIPS FOR MASTERING DIALOGUE

1. Every conversation takes place somewhere specific. Add a bit of action or description once in a while to ground readers in the setting and help them keep track of the speaker. If your characters are sitting in a restaurant, have the waitress stop by or have a patron drop his fork, that kind of thing.
2. Great dialogue occurs in a scene that contains conflict. Two nice characters congratulating each other on a victory isn't nearly as fun as two characters from the winning team who not-so-secretly hate each other's guts. Does one guy pat the other guy's back a little bit too hard during the post-game celebration? Does the other guy use some belittling nickname as revenge?
3. Give two of your characters opposing agendas. Maybe a wife wants to arrive at her office's fancy cocktail party before her boss figures out she's absent, while the husband wants to stay home and watch the last ten minutes of the basketball game. Underlying tension between these two characters will spark great dialogue.
4. Cut your dialogue to the bone. Don't write in complete sentences, and don't have characters say each other's names very often (or at all). Phrases and fragments sound more natural. A good exercise: During revision, cut each line of dialogue in half, but keep the same meaning. I bet you can—every single time.

5. Silence is a choice in dialogue, too. When someone speaks and doesn't get a reply, that means something. Use silence as a tool when you can.

6. Don't let someone talk too long. If a character has a long passage of dialogue—like a politician giving a speech or a newscaster on TV—break it up a bit. Have someone interrupt him or pause to let the character perform an action—drink some water, raise his trophy, etc.

7. Use subtext. The text is about what's happening on the surface; the subtext is what's happening underneath. A great way to keep readers engaged is to have a character apparently talking about one thing when in reality she is talking (and thinking) about something else.

8. Use caution when approaching dialect and accents. When overdone, accents and regional dialects can come across as comic or worse, offensive. Sprinkling a *wee* or *ain't* into a character's speech once in a while is enough information for readers.

9. Make each character sound distinct throughout the entire story. To do this, keep your character's dialogue consistent with her personality each time she speaks. If one of your characters is a bully, have him try to win every conversation. If you're writing dialogue for a stressed-out mother, let her lose it once in a while. If your character is quiet or shy, keep his dialogue short. You get the idea. Make him real every time he speaks.

10. Let your characters say something they don't mean once in a while. People can be contrary when they want to distract someone or when they feel overwhelmed.

DIALOGUE EXERCISE: OPPOSING AGENDAS

Great dialogue happens when two characters have opposing agendas. For this exercise, start fresh. Imagine a new essay idea or short story in your mind. Your idea must include two people in conflict. Each wants something, but only one of them will get it. Maybe you'll write about a couple on a house-hunting trip, or maybe you'll write about two people in love with the same person.

Think about what these two people would say to each other if confronted with their opposing agendas. Would one of them threaten? Trick? Seduce to get her way? What words would she use to get what she wants?

Take fifteen minutes to write this verbal confrontation. Make sure to add enough character movement and setting to prevent it from becoming two talking heads on the page.

9

THEME

Stories and essays are about people undergoing experiences. These experiences—their nature and the effect they have on the people involved—will cause the reader to draw conclusions. These conclusions are your themes. And your themes are what your writing *means*.

It's a writer shining a flashlight on some aspect of life and letting the reader see what's there. A theme is the central idea explored by your work, a message you leave in your wake.

A theme can be as short as a word or as long as a sentence. Some possible themes:

- grief
- societal pressure complicating marriage plans
- a difficult childhood
- the quest for food and shelter
- the value of friendship
- homesickness
- coming of age
- man vs. nature
- love is blind
- good vs. evil
- unrequited love
- power corrupts
- claim your own future

- the futility of war
- the necessity of war
- the nature of happiness
- blood is thicker than water
- money can't buy happiness

A great way to study theme is to read widely. Think of the last book or essay you read or even the last movie you watched. Ponder the longest scenes, main conflict, and the epiphany. The epiphany moment is when the main character has a major realization. It's usually a sudden intuitive perception of his situation in relation to the main conflict.

Next, ask yourself what these moments suggest about the human condition. What lessons do they teach? What conclusions can be drawn? What did the story make you feel?

How does this help you improve your short story or essay? The choices you make in identifying your own theme will strongly influence how you revise your written work. Theme will help you make sense of your first draft and help you make decisions about what to keep and what to delete.

You might start writing a piece with a certain theme in mind, but you don't need to. Themes tend to emerge as you write. It won't likely be until the editing stage that you even begin to recognize the themes you've developed. Themes are so closely tied to human nature that it's almost impossible to tell a story without a theme of some kind, so don't worry; you'll have one.

....

"When you hear the word 'theme,' you may groan internally—isn't that the old 'moral of the story' we'd get from Aesop's fables? Well, in a way, yes, it is. But Aesop was onto something. He disguised the meanings of his tales by making them about animals rather than about people. In this way he ... disguised his critical intent from the society he satirized. He created metaphors about human behavior by showing action and reaction. That is

what authors do all the time—particularly with theme. Think of the plotted story as what the reader perceives on the surface, while the theme is the deep-sea creature felt swimming in the dark depths somewhere far beneath. It tells us not what you wrote about but why you wrote it."

—SAVANNAH THORNE

DIGGING FOR YOUR TRUTH

If you've already completed the first draft of your story or essay, you'll have an easier time identifying your theme and using it to improve your second draft.

Let's say that you've completed an essay draft about that time at Lake Pleasant when your sister almost drowned. You've shown the family car trip that led to the campsite, your family setting up camp the first day, and then the actual incident where your sister fell through the rotted wooden dock and was trapped—barely breathing in the small space between dock and water—bobbing for her life.

As you study your prose, you notice that you've portrayed your father as an organized camper. Your sister, the daredevil of the family, talks about practicing holding her breath underwater at the local pool (which you explain was what your father did when he was a kid). And at the end of the essay, your father saves your sister because you alert him by blowing on the whistle he put around your neck—something he gave you to use if you got lost while exploring the woods.

You might look at these three items and decide that your theme is "always be prepared" or "father knows best." Either decision will help you edit your essay.

Your next step is to focus the essay on this singular theme, refining your storytelling so that much of the essay relates back to the theme in some way. This is a great way to add depth. The repetition of thematic elements will naturally pile up, creating resonance within the story.

If you choose the theme "always be prepared," you can go back to the car trip and show a bit more about how your family prepared for the trip. Maybe your mother always packs a gallon of water for emergencies and sandwiches, too. Then you could also show more detail when the family arrives at the campsite. Perhaps you could show something that happened when you weren't prepared, like the wood being too wet to start a fire—so you ate cold soup instead. This adds a nice sense of balance to your story and also foreshadows the near-drowning by showing readers that not everything will go well for your family on this trip.

If you decide to embrace the theme of "father knows best," you could make your father the focal point and revise the whole story accordingly. You could give him the majority of the dialogue during the car ride. Maybe he advises you and your sister about the proper way to build a fire and then tells you that you'll need to wake up at 6 a.m. so that you can enjoy the sunrise—because a morning sunrise is really the best thing about camping. Perhaps you add your own internal dialogue during the car ride, giving the reader a sense of how you feel about your father and his long-winded "my way is the only way" view of the world. You could lead readers through the setup at the camp through this lens, too, showing your father and his need to have things done a certain way. The readers will see him insist that you wear that embarrassing orange whistle around your neck.

Both of these revision choices will vastly improve on your original idea, and that's the whole reason to stop and think about theme. When you have a theme, you are able to make editing choices with confidence and reveal the best version of the story.

....

"I teach students how to flesh out themes in the work they read for my courses, but thinking about themes and sub-themes is the last thing I want to do as I'm composing those first important 'gut' drafts of a story or essay. That said, taking time to deeply consider themes can make both the revision and

editing processes enlightening and productive experiences. For example, I've written many pieces about my son and husband and their favorite sport: motocross. Each of these pieces has the overarching theme of 'sport' and, more specifically, 'envy' (how much I envy their talent and technique). However, when I decided to submit my work to the Prairie Schooner's Sports Shorts series, I had to think about what makes this sport stand out from others—what are some sub-themes that set it apart? I came up with 'daring' and 'fearlessness in flight.' I looked through drafts I'd written, and I chose a piece that illuminated these sub-themes that weren't necessarily present in other pieces I'd written. Furthermore, motocross is known for its memorable and exhilarating sounds, so I amplified the 'sound' in the piece using words like 'yammering' and 'hammering' that echoed the actual sounds on the track."

—JOLENE MCILWAIN

TEN TIPS ON PRESENTING YOUR THEME

1. Theme is not cut and dry, and it shouldn't be overly obvious. If you're working on a theme involving sacrifice, you don't want to have all of your characters making a sacrifice in every scene. Theme works best when it's subtle.

2. Since themes can contain messages and morals, make a conscious effort not to force your personal beliefs and values on your readers. Most readers don't like writing that preaches at them. In fact, some themes work best when they work as questions and the reader gets to experience contrary viewpoints. For example, we all accept that stealing is wrong, but we feel differently when a starving child steals a loaf of bread.

3. Theme and subtext are powerful allies. Find places where your characters can have hidden agendas that illuminate your theme, or use subtext in your dialogue to deliver your message.
4. When it comes to themes, raise questions but don't feel the need to answer them. Leave the reader some room for his own interpretation.
5. Use symbolism to convey your theme when you can. If, for instance, your symbol is an object, you're pointing the reader toward your theme whenever it appears in your story.
6. Characters sometimes voice the theme early in a story or essay.
7. Characters themselves can embody your theme. The things they do can suggest your central theme.
8. Your theme can be implied in your title.
9. Weave your theme into the main conflict of the story for maximum impact.
10. Your readers don't need to think about theme to enjoy your story. They'll get a sense of your overall meaning, even if they aren't searching for it.

EXERCISE: DISCOVER YOUR THEME

You may see one clear theme emerge in your early drafts, or you might find that a handful of themes pop up. Identifying these themes will help you understand your work better and allow you to make smart editing choices.

For this exercise, select one of your unpolished pieces of writing. Sleuth out possible themes lurking in the prose by thinking about these questions:

1. What was your original purpose for writing this essay or story?
2. What does the main character's arc say about human nature?
3. Is there a particular phrase or sentence that resonates strongly?
4. What happens in the pivotal scene?
5. Are there repeated symbols anywhere in your piece? What do these symbols mean to you?

6. What does the main character's epiphany reveal?
7. What are the longest passages about?
8. What does the main conflict tell you about society?
9. Is there a lesson to be learned from this piece?
10. What can you do to clarify the piece's meaning?

List as many themes as you'd like. There's no limit; you're just examining your prose. Later, when you're ready to begin your next draft, circle the three themes that you think most closely relate to your essay or story's main point. Use those themes to guide you toward one idea that unifies your entire piece.

CRAFTING A SHORT STORY

Short stories can be written in any form. They can be funny, scary, dialogue-filled, or sparse. They can fit into a popular genre (such as science fiction, horror, romance, mystery) or no category at all. Published short stories today—in any flavor—contain compelling characters, interesting plots, meaningful settings, significant themes, and literary voice delivered through strong scenes. Studying each of these elements is crucial to writing a publishable short story.

ESSENTIAL ELEMENTS OF A GREAT SHORT STORY

There are five key elements that must be purposefully braided together to create a solid story: character, setting, plot, conflict, and theme. You might start working on your short story by thinking of a unique character or an unusual setting. Perhaps you will see the plot in your head before you write, but you may begin your story without knowing anything up front. Any approach is fine, as long as your last draft includes these five essential elements. Let's take a closer look at each of them:

1. **CHARACTER:** A great focus character is someone interesting enough to watch for the length of the story. Your main character can be

quirky or quiet but never boring. Maybe she says hilarious things or lies for no reason. Let your readers see inside her and identify her motivations.

2. **SETTING:** Your story's time and place must be more than window-dressing. Have your characters walk through a world that amplifies the theme and mood of your story. For example, the weather might change along with the main character's challenges, or you might set your story in a cubicle-filled office to reflect the main character's feelings of being boxed in.

3. **PLOT:** The series of events that take place in your story must relate to a central conflict. If you're writing about two neighbors who are both vying to seduce the hunky new UPS guy, let your readers see their specific attempts at this in real time, starting with small actions and building to bigger moments as the story unfolds.

4. **CONFLICT:** The struggle between two people or things in your story (man vs. man, man vs. nature, man vs. self, man vs. society) is a wonderful thing for readers to experience. They're nosey. Conflict keeps them turning the pages, wondering how the plot will escalate and what the consequences will be for the characters. Dish out conflict bit by bit, and build to a climax. Let readers worry, and then make them worry even more.

5. **THEME:** The central idea doesn't need to be revealed explicitly anywhere for readers to pick up on it. Your theme can shine through in small moments between characters or during elaborate car chases. It is the purposeful way you tell the story's events that will broadcast your theme.

Structuring Your Short Story

The basic recipe of a short story looks like this: A protagonist has a goal or desire. Conflict brings about a change or epiphany in that protagonist, and the ending alters the protagonist's character and/or life. More simply, a short story has a goal, a problem, and a conclusion.

Lucky for us, there are hundreds of ways to convey story structure in short fiction. You can include flashbacks or go backwards in time through the entire piece. You can tell your story from any point of view, including animals and inanimate objects, or you can be an omniscient observer. You can be a reliable narrator or an unreliable one. Anything goes; don't hold back. Your challenge in a short story is to give readers a sense of complexity, even if your story is only one-hundred words long.

Tension and conflict overlap in a short story, but they are two separate tools at your disposal. Conflict is the tangible problem your character is trying to solve, and tension is the delicious way you dole out information about your character dealing with that conflict. Tension is a cocktail of anticipation, uncertainty, and reader investment.

To heighten the tension throughout, vary your sentence length. Use purposeful dialogue to express unease, and minimize exposition (action-only passages exude tension).

Short stories don't require the same kind of wrap-up that novels do. Yes, you need a purposefully written ending, but don't limit yourself. Anything goes here, too. Your conclusion should release the tension in an interesting way, and create a mood that lingers with your readers. The conflict may or may not be resolved.

....

"Well-written short stories begin as close to the climax as thematically possible. The art is in the immediacy—how that first line, or hook, draws you in. The tension of the moment makes the hair on your neck stand up. You keep reading because you know something is coming. You are worried, and the characters are worried, too. Then, boom. Not every climax is a direct lightning strike, however. Sometimes it is a quiet or ambiguous moment that leaves you wondering. You see the strike in the distance or watch it dance across the sky. Then after you finish reading, you're still counting the seconds—one-Mississippi, two-Mississippi, three-Mississippi—and you wait for the distant crack of thunder. If your writing does not have that urgency, find the exact moment before the lightning hits in your story and linger there. Make your characters and readers worried. Make them look up to the sky and wonder what is coming."

—BRIANNE M. KOHL

How to Begin Writing Your Short Story

Every great short story revolves around a compelling character. Readers want a hint at what your character looks like, but don't stop there. Your audience needs to know what this main character wants and needs. They also need to know what is at stake for this person if he doesn't achieve his goal. Will your main character lose his loved one? A job? The chance to visit Rio?

Show this person's nervous habits, his posture, or the way he walks. Make every detail matter to this person's overall character. Tell your readers something about the character's physical appearance that reflects who he is as a person.

The following exercise is intended to get you thinking about characters and their desires:

1. Imagine a character you might like to use in your story. Write down five things that you know about this person: a like, a dislike, a hope, a fear, and his profession.
2. Now let's think about this character's desires. What is your character's goal right now? Perhaps he wants the cute girl from the bakery to go on a date with him, or maybe he wants to be accepted into Harvard. Maybe your character wants both of those things. Think of five things this character could desire right now. Whatever it is, big or small, jot it down.
3. Take a look at your list of five character wants. Beside each character goal, write a few sentences that reveal what would happen if the character doesn't get what he wants—and be specific. For example, if your character wants to date the bakery girl, perhaps the stakes

are pretty high. Maybe he's got a bet with a friend about dating her. Maybe if he fails to get her to go on a date with him, he will have to shave his chest live on YouTube. Each one of the goals you've given this character should have interesting consequences. Be creative, and most importantly, be specific.

4. Take a look at your list of characters and their desires. Any of these can be the spark for a terrific short story. Choose the one you like best, and begin.

Characters usually have agendas. The main character's agenda is the one your readers will learn the most about, but most characters will enter a scene with their own goals in mind. Use this same exercise to flesh out the desires of the other characters in your story.

....

"Bear in mind that as you develop as a writer, as you learn about the craft, you will have more resources to draw on, greater skill when it comes to getting that idea, that story, that moment in time on the page. It always falls short—what I hold in my imagination and how I see it—well, it's never quite there [on the page] exactly as I see it. But then your reader[s] comes along, and they bring their imagination, their life experience to your words, and in a sense they create something with your text. And so the dance begins again ..."

—LISA FUGARD

....

TEN TIPS FOR WRITING A COMPELLING SHORT STORY

1. Write about a character worth watching. He can be gruff or sweet but never dull. Your main character must be worthy of the spotlight you're shining on him. Deepen your characterization by revealing more than his physical appearance. Sprinkle in some hints about

who he is through his furniture choices, the way he talks to strangers, or the way he selects produce.

2. Begin late. End early. The best short stories employ precision and economy. Include only a part of your character's long journey. Give hints about her "before" and maybe even her "after," but tell the here-and-now of your character's story.

3. Veer into the unexpected. Don't stop yourself from writing that idea that sounds a little kooky. Let your story lead you wherever it may go. You can edit later, but don't dilute your story now by editing out potentially interesting bits.

4. Explore something small in fascinating detail. Give your character an unusual trait that matters to the story, and let readers wonder about it as the plot unfolds. For instance, if you give your main character yellow stains on the cuff of her sleeves in the first paragraph and you elaborately describe those stains, your readers are going to notice. They're going to watch for clues about why those stains are there, so make sure you provide some along the way.

5. Layer to amplify meaning. Deepen important ideas throughout your story by restating them in slightly related ways. If the main character is lonely because his wife left him, you might find a subtle way to reflect or enhance his loneliness in his environment (maybe he sees two birds on a branch—one bird pecks the other and flies off), his wardrobe (he loses his shirt buttons one by one over the course of his day), or even his lunch order (his favorite menu item has been banned by the health department).

6. Write compelling scenes. Scenes are those fly-on-the-wall moments in your story where the action is happening right now. Strong scenes engage your readers, so you should rely mostly on scene writing in short stories. When you change characters or time of day, keep your transitions short. Give just enough information to your readers to settle them into the new scene.

7. Use specific words, and choose them with purpose. Tighten up your prose by using strong adjectives. Instead of writing, "James and Amy were still feeling hostility toward each other at the beginning

of the trial," you could write, "James and Amy locked squint-eyes from across the aisle."

8. Study the craft of fiction with fervent dedication. Practice and study, and then practice some more. Not only will craft knowledge make your short stories better; it will actually make writing easier by boosting your confidence.

9. Everything matters in a short story. Every sentence, every image, and every piece of dialogue in a good short story has a purpose. That's something we aspire to achieve when writing longer fiction, too, but novels are long enough to get away with beauty for beauty's sake. In short stories, that beauty needs to mean something. Every word of a short story must drive the narrative to its conclusion.

10. Read. If you want to write publishable short stories, you must read and study published short stories. Read short stories from at least three separate resources. One should be a collection of contemporary standouts (*The Pushcart Prize: Best of the Small Presses* or *The Best American Short Stories*—both publish an annual edition), another should be a collection of stories from masterful short-story writers of the past (*The Art of the Short Story* or *The Best American Short Stories of the Century*, for example), and one should be a stack of recently published literary magazines.

11
CRAFTING A PERSONAL ESSAY

Personal essays are characterized by their sense of intimacy and conversational tone. A personal essay is the author expressing his intimate thoughts and feelings. This can be very difficult, especially when you're revealing something painful, but don't shy away from telling your personal truth. Your audience reads essays because they want to feel a sense of connection with others. When you write from a place of vulnerability, readers see themselves in your situation and understand that their own experiences are universal. They feel less alone. So, be vulnerable on this writing journey. Strip right down to your truest self, and tell your readers what you want to say.

The good news is that you have the freedom to sound like yourself when you write an essay, so use this opportunity for an honest exploration of self. Let your natural voice shine through. Be angry, sorry, shocked, amazed. Be funny or wry. Ponder. Wonder. Examine.

"The personal essay connects writer to reader, soul to soul."

—SUSAN POHLMAN

ESSENTIAL ELEMENTS OF A GREAT PERSONAL ESSAY

When writing a personal essay, you must go beyond something you'd write in a journal or what you'd say at a cocktail party. Personal essays are not a factual retelling of an event from your life but an *examination* of an event in your life. There's an enormous difference between those two things. Consider these five essential elements of a great personal essay:

1. **THE AUTHOR'S PRESENCE:** Speak your truth in a conversational tone. To build a successful essay, you must write about the event(s) and how you feel about what happened. You don't have to be reasonable or rational in your essay. You don't even have to be nice. Don't edit your true feelings out of the piece because you are concerned what people will think of you. Be brave, and speak your mind. It may take several drafts to get to the heart of what you want to say.

2. **A CONNECTION BETWEEN THE WRITER AND A LARGER WORLD-VIEW:** An essay is based on something that happened in your life, but your prose should offer a larger truth as well. Personal essays must resonate with readers. Think about what you want readers to take away from your piece. Do you want to inspire them to take action against injustice? Do you want them to understand why caring for your dying husband was an honor and not a burden? Do you want them to feel the powerful vibrations you experienced on your meditation retreat? Readers can experience all of these moments through your words. Connect your personal reflection to a universal truth about life.

3. **SELF-EXPLORATION:** There is an appealing intimacy created by vulnerability, so don't hold back. Tell your story. Make sure to stop and react along the way. Your readers will explore their own feelings right along with yours.

4. **SHOWING AND TELLING:** Every essay is a dance between narrative reflection and visceral scenes that convey your theme to readers. Essay readers want to know what you're thinking. We've all heard writing instructors advise aspiring authors to show instead of tell.

This essentially means that you should write most of your story as scenes with very few narrative passages. That's terrific advice for many writing projects, but essays require a different balance. Moments of introspection—the necessary emotional reactions to your situation—can only happen in narration. These are the "telling" moments in your essay, and they are essential.

5. **AUTHENTICITY:** In your essay, you don't need to be 100-percent accurate with your details, especially when you're remembering something from your distant past, but you do have the obligation to be reasonably accurate. You are the only one who will remember certain events in your life, but don't stray from what you know to be true. When you show your audience your most authentic self, you are facilitating a connection with your readers.

....

"It's okay to have no clue what you're writing about. You don't have to know to start writing. Just choose a sentence, write it down, and follow it with another one. Writing isn't about telling a story; it's about discovering what the story is as we write it. For instance, a few years ago, I wrote a 19-page essay about different typefaces and how the look of what we write holds emotional meaning. I did rounds and rounds of revisions, and by the time I reached the final draft, it was a 25-page essay about the different kinds of violence my body has lived through. The only thing from the first draft that made it to the final draft was one ampersand. One. &."

—CHELSEY CLAMMER

....

How to Choose Your Topic

Personal essays are often inspired by a moment that changed you in some way. Choose topics that spark emotion. Concentrate on obsessions, heartbreaks, and epiphanies. That doesn't mean your essay needs to be about a terrible tragedy from your life. Great essays can be about small, intimate moments, too.

Your personal essay can be about your first day as a lawyer, that time your sister gave you pot, or the orange cat that's always waited for you outside your local Dairy Queen. It's the individual *you* that matters in essay writing, so be as honest as possible in your prose. If you aren't completely honest, readers will likely pick up on this and question your authority. Therefore, when choosing a topic, ask yourself, "Am I willing to be vulnerable about this moment from my life? Am I willing to be exposed?"

To help you generate some essay-worthy material, I'd like to introduce something I call *memory mining*. Memory mining is the purposeful task of digging through your subconscious and finding moments that matter to you.

We've all had powerful moments happen in our lives. You've experienced some highs and some lows, some surprises and some defeats. You've felt ashamed, you've won awards, and you've fallen in love. Let's explore some of the things that have happened in your life.

Begin with your eyes closed. Think of your childhood. What's the first thing that comes to mind? It probably isn't an entire day or an entire vacation; it's more likely a specific situation. Perhaps you see yourself sitting on that wobbly rocking horse your father carved by hand.

This image has power.

This image pushed past all of the other choices your brain could have showed, and therefore, it could be used in your writing. This moment matters to you, and it's now up to you to figure out why.

Dig deeper: What do you smell? Are you afraid? What year is it? How old are you? Are you happy? Do you know who else is nearby?

....

"Don't dismiss the small moments. They reveal your obsessions. This will offer the best place to find a starting point for your essays. Let your senses guide you and incorporate what you

*feel, hear, see, taste and touch as a part of your narrative arc
and epiphany. Using this approach will not only feel cathartic for
you, but also make the person reading your work feel less alone."*

—RUDRI BHATT PATEL

You are the very best authority on what this moment feels like. You can infer anything you'd like from the images and your reactions. Maybe you'll remember a loss or a victory. Maybe you'll remember some specific rule you were bound to. Whatever comes to you, let it in. Jot it down. Mull it over.

Next, close your eyes again and think of the color green. What image popped into your head this time? Was it your grandfather's farm? The taste of those peppermint candies your Aunt Dora loved? Or perhaps you saw yourself smelling a green scented marker.

This image is another piece of your history that can be used in your writing. How does your grandfather's farm make you feel? Lonely or safe? Did your Aunt Dora give you permission to eat her candies, or did you steal them? Why are you holding that green marker? Were you working on a homework assignment or drawing for fun?

Each of your authentic moments matter because they've pushed up through your thoughts like the first tulips of spring. They are organic, original, important. Grab those moments, and use them in your essays.

Structuring Your Personal Essay

Essays contain a beginning, middle, and end, with a moment of transformation in there somewhere—a turning point for the narrator. The narrative arc of an essay looks like this: The writer examines an event from her life and has an epiphany. That epiphany informs a transformation.

That transformation is what makes a personal essay completely different from a diary entry. Essays are examples of us examining life and learning something from our experiences.

Essays are about a specific moment, but they are also about a larger idea. This idea is the theme (or log line) of the essay. Maybe you want to express "Don't forget to say *I love you*" or "Divorce is hard." Understanding the purpose of your essay will allow you to create a connection between the emotional journey of your story and the plot, enhancing the essay's impact on your readers.

You probably learned the "introduction/body/conclusion" formula in school at some point. It looks like this:

1. Introduction
    a. Opening line: A moment that catches the reader's attention.
    b. Set the scene: Provide some relevant information that settles the reader into your essay.
    c. Convey your point: State your overall theme in a creative way.
2. Body
    a. Supporting evidence: Tell elements of your personal story that relate to your theme.
    b. Conflict: Give examples of increasingly difficult challenges. Increase tension further with the addition of internal or external struggles along the way.
    c. Epiphany: Reveal a moment of clarity that signifies a change or transformation.
3. Conclusion
    a. The moral of the story: Conclude with some reflection or analysis of the events.

This formula is a perfectly acceptable way to write a personal essay, but it doesn't exemplify how much creative freedom you're actually allowed. Today's published essays stretch the artistic boundaries more than ever. Examples include "Son of Mr. Green Jeans: An Essay on Fatherhood, Alphabetically Arranged" by Dinty W. Moore, an alphabetical collection of unusual fatherhood facts, and David Foster Wallace's "Consider the Lobster," which masquerades as a magazine article. Some essays read like a short story or poem. Some incorporate lists or use multiple subheadings. Some essays are mere fragments of thoughts that eventually add up to something wonderful. So instead of worrying about what goes where, focus all of your energy on your content.

....

"Essays are opportunities to pause and chew on the nuances of the human experience. A great personal essay is all about intimacy. The writer takes us on a literary walk through the landscape of the soul [by] sharing struggles or a humorous observation about life."

—SUSAN POHLMAN

....

How to Begin Writing Your Personal Essay

Personal essays are always written in first-person point of view, which means they employ *I, me, you,* and *us.* Example:

> In May of 1999, I visited my town's annual carnival, where I met a fortune teller who told me I'd fall into an abyss. I still don't know if she meant my marriage to Henry or that sinkhole that swallowed my Honda.

Personal-essay writing requires you to dig for the truth about the topic you've selected, so let your excavation process be whatever it needs to be. You might begin with a clear idea of what you'd like to say, but chances are, some other related idea will take over most of your paragraphs during the first draft. Let it happen. Follow that new idea without judgment, and see where it leads you. Essay writing is about exploring your truth. Don't block yourself from making interesting connections. Let your most honest self speak up.

When you've finished your first draft, reread your prose and hunt for the most interesting descriptions and emotionally charged moments. These hint at what you really want to say on your subject. Ponder ways to deliver a relatable truth that will resonate with your readers. Zero in on repeated or related themes. Circle them. When you've got a tight grip on your theme, grab it and don't let go. Revise your essay with this new, clearer focus in mind.

TEN TIPS FOR GETTING IT RIGHT

1. Be vulnerable. Personal-essay writing requires your most honest self on the page. Whenever you feel yourself hiding behind vague details or skipping the difficult parts, stop and reconsider. The hardest things to admit to ourselves make the best personal-essay material.
2. Offer a universal theme. Readers want to experience connection when reading personal essays. There's something about your experience that will resonate with readers on a visceral level.
3. Let your voice shine. Individuality matters in essay writing. Showcase your cadence, your careful word choice, and your overall style on the page.
4. Tell the outer story and the inner story. The outer story is the event. The inner story is the emotional journey. Show readers something that happened and also how it changed you.
5. Show *and* tell. There is a need for narration in essay writing. These "telling" moments allow readers to watch you ponder your situation. Use both scenes and narration to write a great personal essay.
6. For creative nonfiction, include more showing than telling. If you intend to write a creative nonfiction essay, include more scenes than narrative in the overall balance of the piece.
7. Tell the truth artistically. A personal essay is your version of the events that happened, not an exact retelling. Rely on all of your storytelling skills to convey your truth, and edit where necessary.
8. Take care with characterization. You know the people in your own life, but your readers do not. Remember to present fully realized people with agendas, unique speaking styles, and backstories.
9. Layer to amplify meaning. Deepen the impact of important ideas throughout your essay by reinforcing them in a variety of ways. Mirror your theme in a song on the radio or through the description of the weather.

10. *Read!* If you want to write publishable personal essays, you need to read them. You'll find hundreds of essays available online at places like *The Huffington Post, The Sun, Narrative,* and many other publications. Read notable essay anthologies like *The Best American Essays of the Century* and *The Norton Book of Personal Essays.* Study the style of well-known essayists in collections like Roxane Gay's *Bad Feminist* and Leslie Jamison's *The Empathy Exams.*

"I'm a lover of juxtaposition. I'm a fan of putting two words, two details, two images, or [two] events next to one another and let[ting] them tell my story. This isn't necessarily a thematic approach but an intuitive one. Revising is an act of patience and observation. Before I can fully figure out an essay's organization, I have to write out anything and everything, then take the essay apart, then puzzle [it] back together, then do more extractions, and then add in more writing. Once I think I know the best order for my essay, I let it sit for a bit, then do it all over again. Wash. Rinse. Repeat.

"It's a matter of testing things out and seeing what order creates a more powerful impact. ... We experience and perhaps think about stories chronologically, but our understanding of them is not always linear. Our lives might march forward, but our brains loop around the past and create meaning. It is this narrative of meaning that we must go after in all of our writing because a killer story isn't about what happened but how we tell the story of it. So write it all out, and then listen to what that writing has to say. Then revise accordingly. Wash. Rinse. Repeat."

—CHELSEY CLAMMER

12

FINDING YOUR WAY TO A BEST FINAL DRAFT

First drafts, final drafts, and the work done in between can be daunting, but to have the best chance at publishing success, you need to edit your short stories and essays until they shine bright. Employ every craft tool you have, and revise, revise, revise!

Take a moment to look at the writing projects you'd like to see published. Are they early drafts? Mid-drafts? Or are they fully formed, edited pieces of prose? Writers produce a lot of drafts, but not everything we create should go out the door. Be honest. Are your essays and short stories ready for an editor's eyes? If not, keep working.

Why be so careful? Because most magazines' editors won't suggest an edit if your prose isn't ready for print. They just don't have the time to invest in the developmental process with writers, even if they'd like to. Their submission piles tower beyond reason. Instead of offering suggestions, editors will have to send you a rejection letter if your prose doesn't yet meet the level of execution they require. So give yourself the very best chance at publishing success. Finish the piece to your best ability before you send it anywhere. Have someone else read it and give you comments. This way, you'll have no regrets when you send your prose out the door.

A GREAT FIRST DRAFT

The best way to ensure a great final draft is to have a complete *first* draft. That doesn't mean you need to have a *beautiful* first draft. It's quite the opposite, in fact. To ensure a maximum dose of creativity in your prose, you must allow yourself to be messy with that first draft. Get your ideas on the page, no matter how rough they feel at the time.

Don't stop and inspect your words until the writing slows down. Then look at your overall idea, and decide if you've completely explored your thoughts. If not, keep writing.

Many of my first drafts don't actually make it past this early stage. Common problems include stories that sound more like character studies or essays that never find a focus. I write for a while before making any judgments about a piece, but eventually I consider my options: Should I keep writing or move on?

If I feel the prose is interesting, I stay with the work. I push past the narrative problems and explore thematic elements. I elevate my word choice and sensory details. I revise and revise, and then I revise again. And then I send the story to my critique partners and let them chime in. After that, you guessed it, more revisions.

If I don't feel that an early draft has enough of a spark to support the amount of work it will take to achieve a final iteration, I tuck that piece into a drawer and walk away. Maybe I will come back to it after a few months and give it another round of editing.

Here's something interesting: Every time I go back and read a piece that just doesn't have what it takes to go all the way, I find something worth saving in those pages. It's usually something small, a gem in the prose that I can use for a different project. Maybe I resurrect a quirky secondary character, or perhaps there are only a few good lines—a fabulous title, even. Revisiting and assessing your work is always useful. Those "almost drafts" have a purpose on our creative journey. Use them wisely.

Early drafts and midway drafts are necessary pieces of writing that can lead to publishable prose, but they themselves are not publishable pieces. Character studies are not short stories, and essays need to make a point. Don't stop the evolution of your work before you've reached the very last draft. If you can't push a piece to the finish line, set it aside.

Edit from the Outside In

When revising your short story or essay, the most economical way to approach your task is to tackle the big-picture edits like story arc and characterization first. Then move on to items that require a narrowed focus, like word choice and dialogue. Edit for grammar and punctuation last. Here's a list of things to consider while revising your prose.

Check the big-picture items first:

☐ Is this the best setting for this story?

☐ Is this the right focus character for this story? Is she interesting or flawed?

☐ Is there a clear narrative arc, including a turning point and an epiphany?

☐ Does every scene belong in this piece?

☐ Do the secondary characters add to the overall story?

Next, move in closer:

☐ Is the balance between narrative and dialogue appropriate for this piece?

☐ Is the main character's goal or desire clear?

☐ Is the story paced to keep the audience invested? Is there rising tension?

☐ Are the transitions smooth?

☐ Is the setting clear and visceral?

☐ Does each character's dialogue sound authentic? Does the dialogue move the story forward?

☐ In each scene, is the reader a fly on the wall? Can you see and feel these moments?

☐ Does your voice shine through?

Last, zoom all the way in:

☐ Is the first sentence a strong hook?
☐ Can you omit any clichés?
☐ How's your grammar? Spelling?
☐ Is every detail specific and visceral?
☐ Do you have any repeated words in close proximity?
☐ Are all of your adjectives and adverbs necessary?
☐ Is your POV consistent?
☐ Are your tenses consistent?
☐ Are your dialogue attributions smooth?
☐ Does your language evoke all five senses?
☐ Have you deleted every unnecessary word?
☐ Does that last line resonate with readers?
☐ Does the title pull the audience into the prose?

"Sometimes a story or an essay can meander along for several paragraphs or even pages before landing somewhere dynamic. Make sure your opening pages aren't a form of 'throat-clearing.' Sometimes the story begins on page 3. This is often clear when you read it after putting it aside for some time. Trust your instincts."

—LISA FUGARD

Titles

Write this down: *Essay and short-story titles matter.* They are the gateway to your prose. Don't settle for a lazy or boring title. You want to entice readers to stay a while and see what you have to offer in the following pages.

When selecting a title, be purposeful and specific. I like to dig through my work for a sentence or phrase that stands out. You can also pick a specific item from your work, something that has meaning in your story. Maybe you state your theme as a title. For inspiration, flip through the pages of any literary magazine and read the titles you see there. What you won't find: boring titles.

Editors see your file name when you submit your prose, so it's best to have that file name reflect your title in some way (or *be* your exact title, in my opinion, even if it's long). Many writers change their story title more than once during the revision process. When your story is complete and you've settled on the perfect title, remember to go back and change your file name, too.

....

"I have often found that the title of a piece changed with every draft and that when I land on the final title, it usually signals that I'm on the final draft. It's not as sacred as changing your name or the name of your child. Titles can change as your theme evolves. That's good. That shows progress, not disloyalty."

—STUART HORWITZ

....

Read Your Work Aloud

One of the best ways to find fixable moments in your prose is to read your draft aloud. You don't need anyone to sit and listen. Just talk to your computer screen or your dog, if he's nearby. You'll hear the places where you stumble, and you'll find some typos.

Try listening for those areas where you speed up your speech and the places where you slow down. What you have on the page should convey that same cadence. When you speed up, ensure that the sentences in that section are short and tight so that readers will speed up, too. When you slow your speech, check whether the phrasing would compel the reader to slow down and look more intently at the action. If not, can you revise it?

For an even more enlightening experience, have someone else read your work aloud to you. When she trips over a word combination or a garbled sentence, make a note on your copy but don't interrupt her. Let her get to the end as smoothly as she can. Take notes about her cadence. Where did she speed up? Is there something that made her laugh? Was she supposed to laugh? Did she read your last line with confidence or confusion?

When to Show Your Work to Someone Else

If you really like a piece of your writing but you're not absolutely sure that it's ready for an editor's eyes, my advice is this: Don't submit it yet. Instead, find someone else to read your story. Other writers, critique group members, and writing instructors are all your partners in polishing your prose. You can find many potential helpers in online groups like WordTango, Scribophile, and Zoetrope Virtual Studio, among others. Share your work, and let people help direct you to your final draft. Ask them where they think you can improve your prose, and then make any changes you agree are necessary.

You don't want someone else rewriting your work, of course, but writing is an act of communication. We need to know that our stories make sense to our readers. We need to know which part of our essay punches readers in the gut and which part needs a tweak. We need to see the story the way a fresh reader sees the story, warts and all.

Critique partners are colleagues who are working on projects they'd like to see published too, so they understand your goal, and they know how to help. Writing instructors can provide terrific help with editing, too.

....

"You may have heard all good writing requires a bit of thievery—sometimes we learn from the greats by stealing from them. The same goes for creating a critique group. In most cities, you can find free (or low-cost) writing groups on websites like Meetup or Craigslist ... and then steal the good eggs. I did this for years:

Every time I moved to a new city, I would find a fiction group on Meetup, go to one or two events, dislike 80-90 percent of the writing being workshopped (a preponderance of bird poems), and then find the one or two writers whose work I really connected with. I didn't even feel a smidgen of guilt when I spirited these gems away to create our own awesome critique group."

—BREE BARTON

Critique Groups

We could all use a supportive tribe of writers in our lives. Sharing pages with two or three other writers each month is all you really need to grow as a writer. Let's look at the *who, what, when, where,* and *why* of critique groups:

WHO: A productive critique group consists of anywhere between two and six writers. The ideal number of partners is really up to you, but if you invite more than five, then you'll need to schedule a large block of time for each session.

Feel free to mix genres and writing styles. Welcome any creative writer who is working on short prose; essayists and poets can give you valuable feedback on a short story. They work with language every day. Any writer is a skillful reader and part of your target audience.

You can meet potential critique partners at libraries, writing classes, and conferences. I met one of my own critique partners through a class, and she brought in two more writers she'd met through other avenues. Sometimes you'll even meet a writer at a non-writerly event, like a cocktail party. Writers are everywhere.

WHAT: A critique group gathers so that each participant has the opportunity to receive quality feedback about his prose. Typically, each writer will submit an essay or story to the group a few days ahead of time via e-mail. Every participant then reads each submission and brings notes about it to the group meeting.

You're going to want to establish some rules for giving feedback. A common structure looks like this: Each reader must provide you with three things he admires about your prose and three things he thinks can be improved. Writers do not like being told how to fix their stories, so don't be one of those people. Instead, give your partners very specific information that will help them make choices about improvements.

For instance, saying "I didn't get it" doesn't help a writer because it doesn't give her enough information to make an informed edit. Instead, saying "The ending felt unfinished" is a tangible clue for the writer to explore. She might even ask you to clarify.

It's up to you to evaluate the feedback you receive. Take what feels right to your story, and leave the rest. You don't have to make all of the changes your readers suggest. Tip: If you hear similar comments from a number of readers, then you know that a piece is worth reexamining.

WHEN: Meet regularly. Sharing your work every other week or even once a month is enough to help you improve your writing skills and polish your prose. When all critique partners participate regularly, everyone benefits.

WHERE: Meeting around someone's dining room table is a fantastic way to get together, but you can use large tables found at most coffee shops and libraries, too. You don't need to live in the same city, either. You can share work through e-mail any day of the week.

My three critique partners live in three other states. We share our work via Google Drive, in a document section reserved specifically for the four of us. We make notes on each other's manuscripts, then e-mail each other with any further questions or clarifications.

Google Drive is easy to use and allows us to see notes from all participants at the same time. I'd recommend it for any group that isn't able to meet in person. Other great choices for sharing documents include Dropbox, iCloud, and MediaFire.

WHY: Critique groups have deadlines, which keep you productive. You receive helpful feedback at the meetings so that you are able to improve your prose during your next revision.

Your critique partners will get to know your writing habits, good and bad. They will high-five you when you nail a sentence and challenge you when you've become lazy on the page.

Here is some sound advice from writer/editor Dr. Michelle Lee about getting the most out of critique sessions:

> Sharing your work can be a frightening, challenging, and disappointing experience that leaves you confused and deflated. Over the years, I've walked away from "workshop" or one-on-one exchange sessions feeling like I need to gut everything in my story to the studs. I've walked away with ten different opinions on how to revise and no clue which one is right.
>
> However, because of these moments of creative paralysis, I've figured out three key strategies to harvest specific and helpful feedback from critique partners, suggestions that will inspire, rather than overwhelm:
>
> 1. Only share with people you can trust to give you ideas in ways you can handle. Your best writer-friend may be the perfect person to chat about a recent *Writer's Digest* article on the technical ups and downs of plot, but he may be abrasive or aggressive when pointing out the particular flaws in yours. Be honest with yourself: Do you need a spoon full of sugar to help the medicine go down? Or can you take it straight out of the bottle, sour as can be?
> 2. Direct the working session. When you send your draft to your partner, attach a list of purposeful, meaningful questions or issues you want addressed. For example, never just simply say, "Tell me what you think!" You will get either a cheering squad or firing squad in return. Focus the reader's keen eye. Maybe you want to ask, "Does the protagonist seem flat in the poker scene?" or "I'm worried that I am repeating myself. Does it seem that way to you?" Or maybe you write, "The backstory seems to slow the pace—should I add dialogue to make it go faster?"
> 3. Only share your work when it has "legs." Try to wait until your story has a solid frame before giving it to a reader for feedback. This way, you can have a confident conversation about your intentions as

a writer and the motivations/actions/journey of your characters. You will also be less likely to buckle under the "crowd idea" if the group-think begins to take your story in directions you don't want.

Hiring an Editor

If you'd like, you can hire an editor to help you polish your short prose. The role of an independent editor varies depending on the type of editing you seek. When you reach out to editors with your short prose, make sure you're working with someone who is familiar with short stories and essays. Also, you'll need to know what kind of help to ask for. You have a choice between developmental editing and copyediting.

Developmental editing includes feedback on big-picture items like pacing, structure, transitions, and dialogue. A good developmental editor for short prose will be someone who understands the expectations of today's short-story or essay markets and reads this type of writing regularly. If she writes short stories or essays regularly, too, then that's even better.

Copyediting is the process of reading your prose and making line-by-line edits for grammar, punctuation, spelling, and sentence structure. The right editor for this kind of work is someone who owns a copy of *The Chicago Manual of Style* or *The Elements of Style* and knows how to whip your sentences into clean and clear, magazine-perfect shape.

EXERCISE: REVISE VIA THEME

One of the most effective ways to enhance your personal essay or short story during revision is to focus on what you're trying to say and then say it better. For this exercise, you'll need to have a solid first draft in hand.

First, study your prose and choose three possible themes for your short story or essay. Write them down on a separate sheet of paper. For each theme you select, write out three sentences that begin with "I." For example: "I want to show the relationship changes that happen when a daughter becomes a mother."

Next, study your sentences and decide which theme best sums up the idea you'd like to convey in this piece of writing. Revise your work with that theme in mind. Give your readers at least three subtle examples of this theme in your prose.

If you have to alter or throw out most of the original piece to accomplish this, so be it. Let your story become a better version of your original idea. As you make editing choices, keep coming back to your theme again and again. Amplify your theme through the dialogue, setting, and the details you choose.

SELLING SHORT STORIES

&

PERSONAL ESSAYS

13

FIVE STEPS TO PUBLISHING SUCCESS

Whether or not you have a final draft completed or are just starting, you may be wondering, *Who wants to publish my writing?*

This can be a tough question, but I'm here to help you figure that out. In the second part of this book, you'll learn how to analyze your finished creative work and match it to a market. You'll understand the difference between genre stories and literary fiction. You'll know if your essay is a piece of creative nonfiction or a different kind of essay and which outlets to query based on that answer. You will create a list of publications that match your written work, and you'll have the tools in place to find homes for every new piece of short writing you create in the future.

Let's take a look at the task ahead. You have a polished piece of writing that needs a good home. You're confident that it's ready to be seen by editors, and you're itching to submit your work. It's time to send out that piece.

You want to get published, though, so let's not rush through the process. There are a few things to take care of before you press that "send" button. There's a cover letter to write and formatting to adjust, magazines to research, and guidelines to read. You'll need to decide about submission options and which rights you're willing to sell.

Over the years I've perfected a five-step system for submitting short writing. This method has landed me nearly eighty bylines in literary, regional, and trade magazines across the United States and Canada. I've been teaching the core of this five-point program for eight years through a class I call Market Coaching for Creative Writers.

Here are the five steps we'll cover:

- Categorize your work.
- Find potential markets.
- Write a cover letter.
- Format your manuscript.
- Submit like a pro.

This entire five-step process falls under the umbrella of marketing, and if that doesn't feel very creative to you, you're right. It isn't. Marketing your writing is the *business* side of this creative life. It's a necessary bridge between your finished work and a publishing contract.

When you're prewriting (journaling, reading, taking writing classes, and engaged in your various other interests), you're opening the doors to writing well. Then while writing your first draft, you're allowing your artistic self a chance to explore an idea, capturing whatever magic manifests itself during the creative process. And when you're editing that draft (three or twelve or maybe fifteen times), you're shaping your creative vision to provide your readers with an experience, a unique, visceral journey.

But while you're marketing your work, you must rein in that creative brilliance and think like a business professional. Luckily, writers don't need to be boring to get published, so keep your personality intact (as long as you have a nice one). Consider every submission a handshake—the first impression of what can become a wonderful publishing partnership.

MARKETING MONDAY

How much time does it take to market your work? More than you might think. It's something you'll need to make room for in your schedule. I market my finished work every Monday morning. I like to call it Marketing Monday.

Each Marketing Monday I review any unsold pieces of writing on my desk. Some have already been submitted (and have logged a few rejections), and others are brand-new stories. Each Monday I review these pieces and make a plan for them. I study potential markets, make new matches, and send that work out the door to viable editors. Choosing even one day a month to tackle your marketing tasks will keep you moving toward your publishing goals.

MEET A FEW OF MY FRIENDS

I'd like to introduce you to three writer friends of mine: Joan, Samantha, and Hershel.

Joan has been writing short pieces about her life for the last two years. Sometimes she writes about her childhood in Alabama or her life as a single parent, but most of her finished essays are attempts to process her mother's death. She finally feels confident enough to send a few of them out the door, but she has no idea where to start.

Samantha knows all about personal writing. She survived a life-changing trip to Madagascar as a teenager, and now she's writing a memoir about her experience. She completed her MFA degree three years ago and is nearing the last draft of her book. Samantha knows she'll need to land a literary agent to get her book into the hands of one of the big publishers, so she's working to build her platform. To accomplish that, she blogs regularly about traveling as a young woman and has prepared a few travel essays that she'd like to see published in magazines. Some of her pieces are serious, and some are funny. One of her essays gives tips on backpacking through Paris while wearing a full leg cast; another essay is a survival guide to using the airplane toilet during a turbulent flight.

Hershel writes for one hour every day, even on holidays. He isn't a fast writer, but he's nearly finished with a novel about a guy who—much like himself—works in the music industry as a sound technician. Hershel writes short stories, too. One of them earned second place in a contest he heard about from a friend. He thinks some of the other short stories he's written are even better than that one, good enough to get published. Two of his short stories take place in a fictional town Hershel calls "Tillview," so he's thinking he might have the beginnings of a short-story collection. He's not sure if he should save those stories for a collection or send them out to literary magazines.

These three generous writers have agreed to let us watch as they work through the following chapters, allowing us to observe them as they make decisions about their publishing options. These three writer friends are especially agreeable to this because they are fictional.

Well, not entirely fictional.

Joan and Samantha and Hershel represent writers I've worked with over the years through my Market Coaching for Creative Writers program. They are composites of authentic situations. They are me and you and that writer you met at a conference last summer. My hope is that hearing their stories and watching them on their journey will help inform your own choices as you progress to publishing success.

You Can Get Published

You have two choices when you finish a piece of writing. You can either hide your prose in a drawer or send it off in hopes of publication. You're leaning toward the second choice, of course, since you're reading this book. But still, you might be nervous.

I get it. The idea of marketing your work can sound overwhelming. There are exact manuscript guidelines to adhere to and long-standing professional standards. There's a large publishing-world vocabulary to absorb and unknown editors to impress.

But I'm here to tell you that marketing your writing is actually very easy. You just need to know how. Remember that list of five steps up there?

- Categorize your work.
- Find potential markets.
- Write a cover letter.
- Format your manuscript.
- Submit like a pro.

You can handle those five steps, right?

Guess what? You don't have to take these steps alone. Joan, Samantha, and Hershel are coming along on this journey, sharing their thoughts as they prepare and submit their work. You'll have a front-seat view of their decisions and motivations, which will help you make choices about your own publishing options.

More editors and published writers have shared their insight on these topics, too. You'll hear advice about the best time of year to submit your work, what to say in a cover letter if you don't have any prior publishing credits, and when you should resubmit to a journal that has previously rejected you. By the end of part two, you will feel like an insider because you will have heard real stories about submitting short prose from people who make the effort every day. Whether you're a Joan, a Samantha, or a Hershel (or any combination of the three), I'll help you find your way. Let's get started.

14

CATEGORIZATION

Categorization is the process of identifying all of the marketing potential in your work. Stepping back to study your manuscript as a sellable piece of creative writing is key to publishing success. You need to communicate what you've written in specific industry terms. When marketing short writing, you need to be clear about what you're offering editors. Did you write a short story, an essay, or an article?

That might sound like an easy assignment, but to sell short prose, you have to know more. What kind of short story or essay have you completed? Some short stories are identified as genre fiction, while others fit into literary fiction. Some essays are creative nonfiction, while others are not. And sometimes you think you've written an essay, but it's actually a nonfiction article.

If you're feeling overwhelmed, don't worry. This section of the book is going to explain the nuances of short prose. You'll learn to identify the potential within your finished writing so that you can maximize your publishing opportunities, no matter what you wrote. First, let's review the types of writing that Joan, Samantha, and Hershel have created.

Joan has a handful of personal essays she'd like to see published. She's worried about the ones she's written about her mother, though. She's not sure if she wants to publicly reveal as much as she has, but she knows the truth about her mother's mental illness could help others. She's considering fictionalizing these essays as a way of keeping her mother's name out of print.

Samantha is working on her Madagascar memoir, and she's ready to submit pieces about her travels in that country along with the funny essays she's written about travel in general. Samantha has been back to Madagascar three times since her initial visit there. She's written about how the political climate has changed in that region and the differences in her experiences as an American tourist there over a decade of visits. Samantha thinks that some of her pieces could be sold as nonfiction articles instead, but she isn't sure.

Hershel has four short stories ready to go. He reads mystery and suspense books when he's on tour with the band, and though his short stories have an air of suspense, he doesn't think he has written *genre* stories. When he is home, he reads political nonfiction and literary fiction, which he thinks influence his work more than his mystery reading does, but he could be wrong. He isn't sure where his writing style fits into the market. Is he a genre writer or a literary writer? Maybe he's both.

CATEGORIZING SHORT STORIES

Short stories are sold with two main pieces of information in mind: word count and genre. But there's much more to know about your stories. There are many distinct categories of short stories in both literary and genre writing.

Word Count

First, let's take a look at your word count. Stories are calculated by counting the number of words in the body of your story, without the title or the heading. The industry calculation is that one page equals 250 words, but for shorter pieces, you'll want to be specific. You can count the words by hand or use your word processor. For programs such as Word and Pages, highlight the body of your prose to check the word count. Then have a look at the following fiction length categories.

MICROFICTION	up to 100 words
FLASH FICTION	100 to 1,000 words
SHORT STORY	1,000 to 20,000 words
NOVELLA	20,000 to 50,000 words

Anything longer than 50,000 words is considered a novel.

Let's take a look at Hershel's short stories since he's the writer with strictly fiction on his desk. Three of Hershel's stories clock in between 2,000 and 3,000 words, and one of them is much longer—nearly 7,000 words. After reading the chart of acceptable story lengths, Hershel is now thinking that he might polish up a mini-story he wrote about his guitar and try to sell it as flash fiction.

Next, Hershel needs to know whether he's written genre stories, literary stories, or both. This will help him decide which types of magazines to approach. As a rule, genre magazines acquire genre stories and literary magazines acquire literary stories, but *consumer* magazines acquire both types of stories.

Sometimes it can be hard to tell what you've got in front of you, and that's how Hershel feels. He thinks his work would fit into a literary magazine, but maybe he should approach mystery magazines instead. He'd like to see his work in print, not just online, but that doesn't help him decide where to submit his stories. Many magazines offer print options. To market his prose effectively, Hershel needs to know exactly what he's offering.

Genre Fiction

Genre fiction refers to stories that fit the traditional genre categories of mystery, romance, science fiction, fantasy, and horror. Genre books are often categorized as "popular fiction" because the stories put an emphasis on entertainment and therefore are very popular with the masses. This is also the expectation when selling short genre stories: They are meant to be enjoyed by a wide audience.

Genre magazines expect high-quality prose and well-developed stories. Genre stories rely heavily on scene writing, the use of specific visceral details, and loads of tension. If you write genre stories, you'll have many outlets for publishing, as long as you meet the plot expectations of this category.

About those expectations: Genre stories are plot-driven tales. I repeat: plot-driven tales. This means that your story must be heavy on action, and that action must be purposefully directed to the reader's expectations of each specific genre. Let's take a look at the expectations for each of the main genres:

- **MYSTERY:** In these stories, somebody solves a crime.
- **ROMANCE:** Romantic love happens between two people; the story usually ends on a positive note.
- **SCIENCE FICTION:** Science-fiction stories feature science and technology. They pose and answer a "what if" question.
- **FANTASY:** Characters in fantasy stories usually have special powers. Magic is the norm.
- **HORROR:** Horror stories must elicit fear or dread.

Literary Fiction

Literary fiction, on the other hand, is a bit trickier to define. Literary stories are highly artistic works. These stories have an emphasis on meaning instead of entertainment, are character-driven instead of plot-driven, and are often experimental in their storytelling.

Literary stories are deep manifestations of the elements of craft. They employ the use of evocative language and thematic purpose; they showcase authentic phrasing and arresting voices; and they contain symbolic, psychological, or metaphysical themes.

One note: A short story can contain elements of a genre category and still be considered literary fiction, as long as the story is written using sophisticated craft techniques and isn't a plot-heavy story. For example, many literary magazines publish literary science fiction, literary suspense, and literary fantasy stories.

Did I Write a Genre or Literary Story?

Still confused? So is Hershel. We've discussed the differences between genre stories and literary stories, but you might be looking at the story on your desk and scratching your head, too. Your story might have a toe in each of these two worlds. You might have a horror story told with poetic prose or a mystery story that is, in itself, a metaphor for the Vietnam War. Hershel is wondering about his stories set in his fictional town of Tillview. They are suspenseful tales about a meteorologist, but he's not sure if they include enough of a plot to sell as a mystery. He'd purposefully used the weather as a metaphor for the meteorologist's relationship with his father, so wouldn't that make them literary stories?

Many writers find themselves in this position. You don't need to worry about finding publishing opportunities. There will be plenty. These genre-crossing stories are popular with readers because they are both tangible and artistic at the same time. You just need to find the right outlet. This book is here to help you make the right decisions about where to send your prose, so let's get a clear answer to the question: "Where should I send my literary/genre story?"

Decide by doing some math. If your story is more than 50 percent plot-based action, then the best bet for finding publishing success is to send it to a genre magazine. If 50 percent or more of your pages are spent on character interiority or highlighting the human experience in some other way, then send it to a literary magazine.

Still not sure? That's okay. Check the voice. If you've employed a lyrical, original, or daring voice, try a literary magazine first. If your prose's style is clear and sparse, try a genre magazine. You can even send it to both markets at the same time.

After reading this far, Hershel is confident that most of his short stories do fit comfortably into the literary market—all except one. He's sure there's one mystery story on his desk, so he plans to send that one to a genre magazine for publication. The others he'll send to literary magazines.

How Much Truth Can a Fictional Story Contain?

Hershel has another question. His longest story is mostly true. He based the main character on himself and wrote about the summer he studied abroad in France, specifically the day he got his first tattoo. The shop and the tattoo artist are still working right there in the same place, not that they'd remember him. Hershel wants to know how much truth a fictional story can contain before you have to call it an essay.

The answer is that you can write about anything that really happened to you and call it fiction anytime you want. In fact, I think all great fiction is born from a writer's own experiences. Usually that experience is only a seed that grows to become its own narrative, but you can write down true events from your life and call them fiction when it serves your goals. Your story can even be 100-percent true and still be sold as a short story, as long as you've used fictive craft elements in your prose. Many creative-nonfiction essays read like fiction, and many are sold as fiction.

The big question to ask is: Why would you want to sell a true story as fiction?

Several of my Market Coaching clients have chosen to sell a true story as fiction because they were trying to gain credibility in the area of fiction and a byline for a short story is a terrific way to do that. These clients had a novel in the works or were planning to begin a novel.

Other writers I know chose to sell their true stories as fiction because they didn't want the people involved in the story to be upset about being mentioned. They made name changes and even gender changes to hide their true identities.

And then there's the group of people who really want to have some distance from the truth of what they're revealing on the page. These writers don't want to point out that this happened to them, but they do want the truth of these human experiences to go out into the world.

There are probably other reasons for selling your true stories as fiction. Examine your personal publishing goals to help you decide how to market your true stories. If it reads like a piece of fiction and you'd really like to sell it as a piece of fiction, then go ahead and sell it as such. You don't even need to add a disclaimer when you do.

An important note: If you're telling 100-percent truth, or a really high percentage of truth, then you're going to want to make sure that the other "characters" in your story would be okay with what you've written. Just because your editor acknowledges that you're calling the submitted story *fiction*, the angry ex-girlfriend you've badmouthed in your prose might not. Change the names of people and places to avoid libeling anyone.

After reading this section, Joan has decided to fictionalize one of the stories she's written about her mother—the one about a day at the carnival when Joan's mother was escorted, drunk, from the ferris wheel—and submit it as a short story. She's planning to change the location from a carnival to the Seattle waterfront where there is a tall seaside ferris wheel. It isn't a far stretch from what really happened, but she might make other changes along the way.

Hershel has decided to go ahead and market his long (mostly true) tale to literary magazines as a short story, rather than sell it as an essay. You can examine your own bank of experiences anytime. Maybe you have a true story in your past that you'd like to rewrite as fiction, too. It can be a freeing and cathartic thing to do.

Short-Fiction Categories: Going Deeper

You know your word count and whether or not you wrote a genre story or literary story. You even know that you can sell your true story as fiction, and you've made a decision about that. It's time to dig deeper. Knowing even more descriptors for your prose will help you make the most viable match to a magazine.

Here are some other, more specific ways that your short story can be described:

- **ADVENTURE:** Action-oriented, usually involve man vs. nature conflict
- **AMATEUR DETECTIVE:** Mystery stories where the protagonist is a detective of sorts
- **CHILDREN'S/JUVENILE:** Intended for a young audience
- **CHRISTIAN:** Driven by an inspirational Christian message
- **COMMERCIAL/MAINSTREAM:** Meant to appeal to a large general readership
- **CONTEMPORARY:** Deal with popular current trends, themes, or topics
- **EROTICA:** Intended to arouse the reader sexually

- **ETHNIC/MULTICULTURAL:** Prominently feature central characters who are black, Hispanic, Native American, Italian American, Jewish, Appalachian, or members of some other specific cultural group
- **EXPERIMENTAL:** Innovative in subject matter or style, unconventional, avant-garde
- **FAMILY SAGA:** Chronicle families' lives
- **GENRE FICTION:** Adhere to specific conventions or expectations, include mystery, romance, science fiction, fantasy, and horror
- **GOTHIC:** Feature atmospheric, historical settings with a sense of foreboding
- **HISTORICAL:** Set in a recognizable period of history that is a key factor in the plot
- **HUMOR:** Writing intended to be funny
- **HYPERTEXT:** Electronic stories where the reader determines the plot's direction by opting for one of many author-supplied links
- **LITERARY:** Sophisticated and technique-driven, emphasize character evolution more than than plot
- **LGBTQ:** Focus on lesbian, gay, bisexual, transgendered, or queer characters
- **MILITARY/WAR:** Stories about the military and war
- **NEW AGE:** Involve astrology, psychic phenomena, spiritual healing, UFOs, and mysticism
- **NOIR:** Hard-boiled detective mysteries
- **SATIRE:** Use of humor, irony, exaggeration, or ridicule to expose people's stupidity or vices
- **SLICE OF LIFE:** Revolve around characters in a mundane situation, offer the reader some illumination about everyday life
- **SOCIAL:** Writing intended to inspire positive social change
- **SPECULATIVE:** The all-inclusive term for fantasy, horror, and science fiction
- **SUSPENSE:** Conjure a sense of anticipation and fear
- **THRILLER:** Arouse a feeling of excitement or suspense, feature heightened situations involving international espionage and violence

- **URBAN FANTASY:** Magical characters (elves, vampires, fairies, etc.) interacting in a modern-day world
- **WESTERN:** Set in the American West, usually between the eighteenth and nineteenth centuries
- **YOUNG ADULT:** Writing intended for an adolescent audience

Some of your short stories will include more than one of these categories, and others will not. Some magazines will mention which of these categories they're currently acquiring, and others will be vague about it. Readers have an appetite for all kinds of writing, so don't worry that you've strayed off the publishable map if you now realize you've written a New Age Horror story or some other unusual combination. There's room in this marketplace for a New Age Horror story. In fact, I'd like to read one myself. If a story is written well, there will be an audience for it.

In the following chapters, we'll go into great detail about matching your specific prose, whatever it may be, to potential magazines, but for now, study the list of possible categories and compare them to your finished short stories. How many ways can you describe your story to an editor?

CATEGORIZING PERSONAL ESSAYS

When you write a true story in first-person point of view, you have a personal essay, but to market your prose effectively, you'll need to understand what type of essay you're offering to potential editors. Is it creative nonfiction or participation journalism? An opinion piece or a biography? There are several types of personal essays, and not every magazine publishes every type of them. It's up to you to understand this category and make smart marketing choices.

Creative Nonfiction

Sometimes a magazine will say they only accept pieces of creative nonfiction. We talked a bit about creative nonfiction earlier, but here's a refresher: Creative-nonfiction essays contain a large amount of scene writing and employ sophisticated storytelling techniques.

All creative-nonfiction essays include accurate, well-researched information while telling an appealing story.

Sometimes they blend statistical fact-based journalism with literary art. Sometimes they are narratives about experiences with grief or a piece of parenting advice that explores our deepest fears. Creative-nonfiction essays can be many things. To identify your own writing as creative nonfiction, check the balance of your scene writing and narrative. An abundance of scenes and the use of fictive storytelling techniques are clear signs of a creative-nonfiction essay.

Did You Write an Article Instead?

Before we look at the different types of essays you can sell, we need to be sure that you haven't actually written an article. The difference between articles and traditional essays is one of the most confusing concepts for newer writers, but the distinction is important. To sell your work effectively, you must understand what you're offering.

Joan is sure that all of her short pieces fit into the personal-essay category, but Samantha has been wondering if she's written a few articles along the way. To help you understand exactly what you've got in front of you, let's take a closer look at the difference between essays and nonfiction articles.

The Personal Essay

A personal essay is based on a personal experience from which you have gained significant meaning or insight or learned a lesson. It can also be based on a milestone or life-altering event. Essay writing is your heartwork, done in your own way, and at your own pace, edited with all of the tools that come along with the craft.

- It's a true personal narrative where the writer describes an incident that resulted in some personal growth or development.
- It is written in first-person point of view.
- It includes dialogue, imagery, characterization, conflict, plot, and setting.

- The writer uses scenes and theme to convey a point. There is a lesson or meaning to the story.
- It is a subjective account where the writer has expressed her feelings, thoughts, and emotions.

Your essay can be about the time you climbed Mount Everest or that time you fell down the stairs. Your subject can also be a personal opinion on an issue such as the garbage strike, crime, or unemployment.

The Article

An article can be based on personal experience and expertise, too, but there are significant differences. Articles are fact-based pieces of writing that involve research. They are not introspective. They are objective pieces of writing that mirror the informational tone of the magazine in which they appear.

The prerequisite for a well-written article is crisp, clean, factual copy. You can't make anything up. These articles might require you to interview a subject. Any facts mentioned must be verifiable. Some categories include parenting, health, travel, author interviews, and music.

Some writers find themselves scratching their heads when they look at their travel essays, wondering exactly where they fit. Samantha is scratching her head, too. She's written several pieces about Madagascar, all completely accurate and factual but in first-person point of view.

The Decision

If you're still wondering whether your essay is really a magazine article, maybe it is straddles both categories. I've had many clients over the years who created awesome prose of this type. It usually happens when someone has written a personal account of how something specific (and well-researched) has affected his life. Some examples: "How Meditation Changed My Eating Habits," "How a Raw Food Diet Saved My Marriage," "How Astrology Landed Me a Job," etc.

If you have more facts than personal history in the piece, selling it as an article will be easier. To do that, you'll need to pitch your article idea to an editor. Later in this book, there's an entire section dedicated to pitching that will help you sell your articles.

If your voice is the highlight of the prose or if the story you reveal has a transformational element, you'll find it easier to sell the piece as a personal essay, even if your piece contains a large amount of factual information. To sell a personal essay, follow the five steps in this book.

There are many of these types of works getting published every day. The line is blurring between strictly nonfiction and essay, creating even more opportunities for writers who have a talent for well-researched heart-work. The way writers take these essays to the market is evolving, too. There are a few markets that actually take pitches for personal essays now, including *Unworthy, BuzzFeed*, and *Narratively*.

Samantha now feels confident that most of her finished essays are personal travel essays, but she does have one finished piece that fits into the article category. She's setting it aside for later. For now, the discussion will return to categorizing personal essays.

Types of Essays

Most editors have a narrow list of the types of essays they'd like to receive on submission. To know which magazines could be a viable match to your work, you first need to know which of the three main categories your essay falls into. Let's take a look at the three main personal-essay categories:

1. **LITERARY ESSAYS:** These essays employ extensive use of literary elements, such as symbolism, style, tone, theme, characterization, and scene-building. Often, these essays are recognizable by their unique or lyrical voice. Many literary essays find homes in literary magazines, but literary essays don't need to be limited to these markets. Essays that appeal to a large market, like those that are humorous, satirical, and nostalgic, can find homes in other outlets, such as regional and consumer magazines and some newspapers.

2. **REPORTED ESSAYS:** (sometimes called Participation Journalism) These informational essays blend a personal narrative with some reporting and statistical analysis. Many travel, parenting, and

political essays fit into this category. Lifestyle magazines and newspapers publish these essays, though some literary magazines do, too. Read *The Huffington Post* and *The Washington Post* for great examples of reported essays.

3. **EVERY OTHER ESSAY:** There are many kinds of true stories being published today: humor, satire, opinion, slice-of-life, nostalgia, reflections, and more. There are endless ways to convey the human experience and many forms you can choose as a vehicle. This third category of essays includes anything you create that doesn't fit into the literary or reported categories. This category of essays has the potential to be published in literary magazines that aren't heavy on literary elements; lifestyle, regional, commercial, and some trade magazines; and newspapers.

Once you study the essay in front of you, make a decision about these three main categories. Did you write a literary essay? A reported essay? Or is your essay some other wonderful thing? Ask yourself, *What kind of magazine have I seen this type of writing in before? Or was it a newspaper?*

Joan has decided that some of her essays are literary essays and some might be considered "other." Samantha's essays fit into two categories as well. Her travel essays fit into the "reported" category, and her humorous essays fit into "other."

Essay Categories: Going Deeper

By now you understand what makes a personal essay different from an article, and you know which main category of essay you've written. You even know whether your essay is a piece of creative nonfiction or not. Now it's time to look at sub-categories. Consider these other personal-essay descriptors:

- **ARGUMENTATIVE:** Attempts to convince the reader to adopt the writer's point of view
- **BIOGRAPHY:** Reveals the personal view of the writer about a notable person

- **CAUSE AND EFFECT:** Explains why or how some event happened and what resulted from the event, lays out the relationship between two or more events or experiences
- **CRITICAL:** Analyzes the strengths, weaknesses, and methods of someone else's work
- **COMPARE AND CONTRAST:** Discusses the similarities and differences between two things, people, concepts, or places
- **DESCRIPTIVE:** Provides details about how something looks, feels, tastes, smells, makes one feel, or sounds
- **EXPERIMENTAL:** Uses an unusual format or layout or unexpected language
- **HUMOR:** Written with a humorous tone, can be satirical or quirky
- **INFORMATIVE:** Teaches readers about a person, place, or event
- **INSPIRED REPORTAGE:** Another term for literary journalism
- **LITERARY:** Use voice, scenes, dialogue, character, tension, theme, and other literary devices to tell the story
- **LITERARY CRITICISM:** Explains how and why a poem, short story, novel, or play was written
- **LITERARY JOURNALISM:** Uses literary elements to tell the story of a person or place, presents a subjective view on a topic and is always a piece of creative nonfiction
- **LYRIC:** Relies on descriptions and imagery to tell something in a poetic, musical, or flowing way
- **NARRATIVE:** Tells a story, the most common type of creative-nonfiction essay
- **PARTICIPATORY JOURNALISM:** Another way to say literary journalism

The magazines you choose to submit your essay to might or might not specify these categories as part of their submission needs. Investigation is easy though. By reading potential magazines with these categories in mind, you'll be able to see which magazines carry each category—and if your essay belongs among their pages.

Take a look at the essays you'd like to send out. Are they literary essays, reported essays, or something else? Do you think they also qualify as pieces of creative nonfiction? And what about those additional categories? How many describe your essay?

CATEGORIZING BY TOPIC

By now you know what main category of short story or essay you've got on your desk and even some additional subcategory information. Those lists will give you great insight into making submission choices, but you shouldn't stop there. You can unlock additional marketing potential by studying your prose like a detective. You've got another group of descriptors to think about: topics.

You're searching for niche-market potential here, so any topic you can sniff out will help—they're a terrific gateway to publication. Does your work contain current events? Have you written about a holiday? Perhaps you wrote an essay about grief or a short story about African elephants. These topics have audiences. There are entire magazines devoted to exploring grief and a long list of magazines that feature nature and animal stories. Once you consider your topics, new opportunities arise.

Great news: The topic of your short story or essay doesn't have to be limited to *just* the main idea. Go further than that. Maybe your grief story is about the loss of a father who struggled with addiction. That's a publishable topic. Maybe your essay is about you and your sisters fighting at the funeral of this same father. Family relationships and sisterhood are also sellable topics.

Let's take a closer look at that short story about elephants. Maybe you've braided the main storyline with another separate topic: an activity that the main character enjoys when he's not taking care of the animals. He might like cooking, or maybe he's a runner training for a race. Both cooking and running are sellable topics. You might even find a trade magazine interested in your story.

Make a list of as many topics as you can. A few possibilities: divorce, gardening, parenting, mind/body/spirit, crafts, pets, travel, outdoor recreation. Think about your workplace. Locations can be topics, too. Consider these setting-related topics: church, the Midwest, trains, seaside, the rainforest.

YOUR TURN: CATEGORIZE YOUR WORK

After studying the information in this section, you're ready to take the first of five steps to publishing success: categorizing your work. You might have several pieces of short writing on your desk or perhaps just one. Gather your polished prose, and get started.

You might prefer to use a legal pad to take notes here, but I like to print out a hard copy of my essays and short stories when I'm working on categorization. I make notes on the first page. Do what makes sense for you.

First, let's look at the obvious: What kind of writing did you complete? Is it an essay or a short story? Are you sure it isn't an article? If you wrote an article, set it aside for now. For short stories and personal essays, keep reading.

Short Story Categorization

You have four types of information to collect about your short story. Note each of these items:

1. Without including the title and byline, what is your word count? Is this piece microfiction, flash fiction, or a short story?
2. Is this a genre or literary short story? If it's a genre story, which type is it?
3. What subcategories can you identify? Examples: historical, humor, romance, LGBTQ, religious.
4. What topics can you identify in this story? List as many as you can. Examples: marriage, grief, dog shelters, antique cars, restaurants, the environment.

Personal-Essay Categorization

You will need to collect five key types of information about your personal essays. For each of your essays, answer these questions:

1. What is your word count? Reminder: Essay word count should reflect only the body of your essay. Don't count your title and subtitle.

2. Which main category of essay did you write? Literary, reported, or "other"?
3. Is your essay creative nonfiction?
4. What subcategories can you identify in your piece? Did you write a narrative essay? A travel essay? Political? Parenting?
5. What topics does your essay contain? Identify as many as you can. Examples: mental illness, sailing, safety, seasons, history, sports.

Keep your category lists nearby for the next section of this book. Now let's take a look at what Joan, Samantha, and Hershel wrote when they worked through this exercise. Each wrote down his/her word count, and here's what they came up with.

Joan is going to work on a fictional version of the ferris-wheel incident, but for now, she'll focus on marketing her essays. She knows that most of her essays are appropriate for the literary market and that two of those are pieces of creative nonfiction. She's also got two essays that fit the "other" category. Joan's topics include parenting, grief, kayaking, gardening, and mind/body/spirit.

Samantha has a few great humor essays, one nonfiction article, and some reported essays to market. She knows that her work doesn't fit into the creative-nonfiction category. Her style is mainstream and satirical. Samantha's topics include Madagascar, relationships, pets, travel, some politics, academia, and organic farming.

Hershel is relieved to answer the "Am I writing literary or genre fiction?" question. He is writing both, which means he'll be marketing some of his stories to literary magazines and one of his stories to a genre magazine. Hershel will be sending consumer magazines both kinds of writing, depending on the vibe of the magazine. His topics include small-town life, natural disasters, religion, insects, brothers, weather, and football. There's no rush when categorizing your work. Allow yourself to step back from the story and see it as a sellable piece of writing. Once you've examined your work and identified all of the selling potential within, you're ready to move on to the next step: figuring out where to send it.

15

WHERE SHORT STORIES & ESSAYS GET PUBLISHED

Once you're confident about how to communicate your writing project, it's time to figure out where to send it. This chapter is going teach you how to discover potential magazines and how to match your work to the right market, but first let's talk about the people at those magazines who will receive your query letter: the editors.

The term editor refers to a couple of different jobs in our industry. There are copyeditors and developmental editors that help your manuscript shine, and acquisition editors who make decisions about what to publish. The editors you'll be working with here are on the acquisition side. They read through submissions and accept or reject prose for upcoming publications.

Editors are our publishing partners. They are not arbitrary gatekeepers tossing rejection letters out with glee. They're far from it. Magazine editors are a specialized team of literary enthusiasts who are devoted to showcasing the best writing they can find. There's no need to be nervous about approaching these people with your writing project; they'll be gentle. They'll respect your time and effort. Editors, in fact, *want* you to approach them. They *need* you to approach them. How else will they find anything to publish?

For an example of the editorial attitude you'll come across in the world of magazines, please enjoy this inspiring article written by writer/editor Chelsey Clammer. This letter was first published in *The Review Review*, an online magazine dedicated to helping writers navigate the world of literary magazines. Back when I was an editor at *The Review Review*, this letter stopped me in my tracks. I still reread it whenever I need a boost.

A MESSAGE FOR WRITERS FROM AN EDITOR: WE LOVE YOU
by Chelsey Clammer

To click is to believe. Believe in yourself. To have confidence that you have a good reason to click. To click is to put yourself out into the world, to make yourself vulnerable to people you don't know, people whose eyes exist to "evaluate" your work. A performance review of sorts. Or, the unhelpful and self-destructive view on all of this: You're about to be judged.

Belief in this pessimistic perspective might deter you from clicking. Best advice I, as an editor, can give to you: Stop those thoughts.

We love you.

Because editors aren't judging you but critiquing your work. These are two totally different things. You may be the coolest person on Earth, but if your writing isn't right for us at this time, it doesn't mean we think you in any way suck. You, my dear, are awesome. We're cheering you on. Keep going.

But we can't do or say any of this if you don't click.

That "submit" button exists for a reason, but it's purposeless if you don't engage with it. I implore you to employ it.

Clicking that button is an act of faith because when you submit you're having some optimism and believing in a number of things, such as:

1. Your writing won't embarrass you.
2. Your writing can reach out to someone else.
3. You have interesting things to say.
4. You can trust a stranger to evaluate your skills and passion.
5. You can trust other people to help your textual, pixelated babies grow.

All of these things are true. So hold on to these beliefs because having an editor judge/evaluate/*consider* your work doesn't have to be terrifying nor a catalyst for anxiety. Submitting, in essence, is starting a conversation. You write, someone reads and then responds, and then you continue the dialogue as you write and edit more. Regardless of the outcome, the point to all of this is that someone is reading your work. Hot damn. This is called sharing. And an editor's response to each submission is full of an act that we call caring.

In fact, there's some mad respect going on in this situation because you're going after your passion and that's awesome. So no matter if publication occurs or not, know that editors will always be cheering you on, will be woot-ing you each time you click.

Put the doubt and anxiety into some metaphorical box, and lock it with some metaphorical key, and throw all that out mentally. Trash all the trash-talking you do to yourself—the *I'm not good enough* and the *no one cares about what I say*. Pahshaw. We want to read; we get excited with each new submission. We want to help share people's words with the world, and so each time a new submission comes in, we're amazed by how so many people write down stanzas and sentences in order to un-silence experiences.

It's beautiful.

Now click.

DEFINE YOUR GOALS

Before digging into finding markets, let's take a few minutes to talk about your writing goals. I know; I know—you're anxious to match your work to a magazine already, but this is important. Your writing goals will influence your publishing decisions from here on out. Take a few minutes to really think about why you're submitting your story or essay to magazines. What do you hope to get out of the transaction? Some possibilities might include:

- having your work read by someone outside of your critique group
- sharing your expertise or experience
- making money

- attracting the attention of a literary agent
- developing a résumé for residency and MFA applications
- promoting your new book
- seeing your work in print
- building your platform
- feeling validated for your hard work this year
- making a name in the world of literary writers

All of these goals are valid, and all of them will require you to make specific, targeted submission choices. To make the right decisions, you need to have a clear idea of what you want when submitting short work now and what you want in the future. Let's revisit the goals of our friends Joan, Samantha, and Hershel.

Joan would like to see her essays published in one of the well-known literary magazines that she's familiar with: *The Sun*, *The Atlantic*, and *AGNI*. She isn't sure if her work is good enough to be accepted there yet, but she'd like to try. She's thinking that she'd like to compile her essays into a book someday, so she'd like to gain the kind of publishing credits that publishers and agents respect. Joan is planning to fictionalize one of her stories, too, so she'd like to reach out to fiction markets. She doesn't have any goals attached to that project, other than to see it published.

Samantha has a completed Madagascar memoir on her desk. She knows that she needs a literary agent to help her get it into the hands of a major publisher. She also knows she must have an organized platform in place before approaching any agents. She's already been blogging, but she'd like to widen her audience with the essays she's written. Samantha wants to reach large audiences. She's interested in seeing her work online and in print—anywhere she can network with other travel writers.

Hershel wants to have at least one of his short stories published in print so that he can give copies of the magazine to a few of his interested friends. His goals right now don't reach much further than that, but he's working on a novel that he might want to see published someday.

He also might like to keep writing his Tillview stories and create a collection. He isn't sure.

Think about what you want to accomplish. What do you hope to achieve with a short story or essay byline today? How would that publishing credit help you achieve your goals?

WHO WANTS TO PUBLISH YOUR STUFF?

Many types of magazines acquire short stories and essays, including literary, consumer, genre, and small-circulation magazines. Some newspapers print essays, especially travel and lifestyle essays.

Literary Magazines

Literary magazines showcase the best writing they can acquire. Some are associated with university MFA creative-writing programs, and others are independently published. Some notable literary magazines include *Granta*, *The Paris Review*, and *Tin House*.

Literary magazines publish weekly, monthly, quarterly, bi-annually, or only one time per year. Many university-based magazines have a short submission window in the fall (September to November, maybe December), while others acquire stories and essays at other times throughout the year. Some accept year-round. There aren't many literary magazines on the shelf at your local bookstore, but there are thousands of them acquiring submissions.

New literary magazines spring up every year while several others close their doors. It can be difficult to keep track of who is doing well and who isn't. One of the best ways to find top-tier magazines is to read the most recent anthologies (*The Pushcart Prize: Best of the Small Presses*, *The O. Henry Prize Stories*, and *The Best American Short Stories*, among others) to see which journal originally published each prize-winning author's work.

Although some well-established journals pay several-hundred dollars for a story or essay, most literary magazines only pay with contributor's copies or a subscription to their publication. However, being published in literary magazines is also about the experience, exposure, and prestige. Literary agents and book publishers regularly read literary magazines in search of new writers.

Consumer Magazines

Consumer magazines reach a big audience, with thousands or millions of readers picking up each issue. Some examples include *Reader's Digest, Good Housekeeping,* and *The New Yorker.* Each of these magazines has a specific, targeted readership. They publish a new issue every month of the year and sometimes every week. You can find consumer magazines at bookstores, newsstands, online, and the grocery checkout lane.

Consumer magazines are open to submissions every month. They select submissions according to an editorial calendar (usually available online) listing upcoming themes for each issue. The large circulation of these magazines translates to well-paying markets, but because these magazines are so well-known, the competition for essay and short-fiction bylines is fierce. Even the biggest consumer publications only buy a story or two for each issue. Some of the best opportunities are in the last few pages, where many of these magazines feature a freelance essay that appeals to their specific audience.

Landing a byline in a consumer magazine allows your story or essay to be read by many people. Consumer magazines are a terrific place to find your readership if you're trying to let people know about a book you already have on the shelf since you can mention the book in your bio at the end of the piece. Although book publishers and literary agents don't usually hunt for new talent in consumer magazines, they'd be impressed to see that publishing credit on your résumé.

Genre Magazines

Genre magazines showcase today's best mystery, science-fiction, fantasy, horror, western, and romance stories. Some well-known genre magazines include *Asimov's Science Fiction, Apex Magazine,* and *Ellery*

Queen Mystery Magazine. These magazines publish weekly, monthly, quarterly, or once per year. Submission periods vary from one genre magazine to the next, depending on the production schedule and magazine's needs.

Many genre magazines are only published online. You can find some in print at bookstores and libraries, but like literary magazines, they don't usually have large circulations, making them difficult to find locally. Genre magazines have a large reading audience, though—including book publishers and literary agents—making them a terrific place to get a byline if you're planning a genre novel. Genre magazines are a low-paying to mid-range market, unless you land a byline in one of the larger publications

Small-Circulation Magazines

Small circulation refers to publications where the printed copies available are under ten-thousand. This can include local advertorials and regional, religious, retirement, hobby/craft, history, and some smaller home-and-garden magazines, among others. Some well-known, small-circulation magazines include *Sun Valley Magazine*, *Sasee*, and *Washingtonian*. You can find small-circulation magazines in your doctor's office, coffee shops, grocery stores, bookstores, record/music stores, artist venues, travel shops, airports, and many other places.

This category of magazines is important because these magazines are especially open to new writers and publish a variety of topics. Much of the content included in these magazines is selected from freelance submissions. This is a terrific place to submit personal essays, travel essays, humor essays and stories, book excerpts, nostalgia pieces, historical pieces, and column ideas.

Submissions are usually accepted year-round at small-circulation magazines. Many work from an editorial calendar, much like consumer magazines. This is sometimes a low-paying market, but small-circulation magazines are a terrific place to gain experience.

Newspapers

Many of the best opportunities for essay writers are in newspapers that have an online, blog-style publication associated with the print edition. *The Huffington Post*, *The Washington Post*, and others publish travel, lifestyle, political, parenting, and some humor essays. Payment varies among newspapers—from no pay at all to competitive rates. Submission windows are open year-round.

MEET A FEW MAGAZINES

I'd like to present a few magazines and show you what they're looking for as a way of getting familiar with what you'll find when you conduct your market search. I've purposely selected magazines that pay with money instead of contributor copies or exposure, but magazines that can only afford to pay you in copies or exposure can be equally important to your writing career. No journal is too small when you're first starting out.

Up-and-coming journals work hard for their writers. They promote work via social media and appreciate it when writers do the same. An underdog today could become the next *Tin House*.

There are thousands of magazines and newspapers acquiring short stories and essays *this week*. Somewhere out there is an editor looking for the kind of finished work you have on your desk. Your task is to sift through the long list of magazines available—paying and not—and make a solid match. This is merely a small sampling of the opportunities available to you (please note that all information was accurate at the date of this book's printing):

1. **BRAIN, CHILD: THE MAGAZINE FOR THINKING MOTHERS:** *Brain, Child* is a consumer magazine that gets 75 percent of its content from writers like you and me. They aren't the typical parenting magazine but something much more elevated. From the editors: "We are more 'literary' than 'how-to,' more *New Yorker* than *Parents*." *Brain, Child* is looking for personal essays about what parenting

does for (and to) the body and soul. They're currently looking for personal essays, humor pieces, and literary fiction between 800-4,000 words long, and they pay competitive rates.

2. **THE SUN:** Established in 1974, *The Sun* is one of the oldest and most respected literary journals still in print. *The Sun* publishes both essays and short stories, with special attention to political, cultural, and philosophical themes. Submissions may have up to 7,000 words. They pay between $300 and $2,000 for each published work, plus a one-year subscription. This is a highly competitive magazine to land a byline in, but there's a great break-in opportunity in the monthly "Readers Write" section. Check a recent issue for current and upcoming Readers Write themes.

3. **GREENPRINTS:** This magazine showcases the human (not the how-to) side of gardening. From the website: "*GreenPrints* is the 'Weeder's Digest.' We publish true personal gardening stories and essays: humorous, heartfelt, insightful, and inspiring." They acquire 90 percent of their content from freelance writers. *GreenPrints* looks for mostly first-person narratives, but they do accept a small amount of short fiction, too and pay between $50 and $200 per published work.

4. **BEAR DELUXE:** *Bear Deluxe* is a national, independent environmental arts magazine that is 80 percent freelance written. They are seeking personal essays of 750 to 4,000 words that engage readers on vital issues affecting the environment. They are also looking for short fiction in these categories: adventure, historical, horror, humor, mystery, and western. They pay between $25 and $400 per published work.

5. **BOULEVARD:** *Boulevard* is a 100-percent freelance-written literary magazine that publishes essays on any topic (especially slice-of-life) and fiction in these categories: ethnic, experimental, mainstream, and novel excerpts. Submissions may not exceed 8,000 words, and they pay between $50 and $500 per published work.

6. **ELLIPSIS... LITERATURE AND ART:** *Ellipsis* is the literary magazine produced by Westminster College. Like all university-based

journals, the taste and style of the magazine can change slightly with each new school year. Check the website for current information about selections. They acquire personal essays, creative nonfiction, and literary fiction all year long. They pay $50 per published work, plus two contributor copies.

7. **HUNGER MOUNTAIN:** *Hunger Mountain* is published by the Vermont College of Fine Arts. They seek traditional and experimental personal essays, rants, and humor, as well as literary short stories. They also have four annual contests. They pay $50 per published work.

8. **AARP THE MAGAZINE:** This magazine features items of interest and importance to people over fifty, but you don't need to be over fifty to write for them. Topics for personal essays vary but might include money, health, travel, relationships, and leisure time. All essays must be under 2,000 words, and they pay $1 per word.

9. **APEX MAGAZINE:** *Apex* is a well-respected monthly magazine featuring dark speculative fiction. They acquire fantasy, horror, and science-fiction stories and pay six cents per word.

10. **ASIMOV'S SCIENCE FICTION:** *Asimov's* is one of the best-known science-fiction magazines in the country. If you'd like to be read by book publishers and literary agents, *Asimov's* is a great place for a byline. They also accept fantasy and humor stories. Submissions must be between 750 and 1,500 words, and they pay eight to ten cents per word.

11. **WOMAN'S WORLD:** This weekly magazine covers pieces of interest to women with a short story in each issue. They acquire romance and mainstream stories of up to 800 words and mysteries of up to 1,000 words, and they pay $1,000 per published work.

12. **THE IOWA REVIEW:** This magazine acquires stories and essays for a general readership. They are looking for personal essays and mainstream short stories of any length and pay eight cents per word.

13. **NEW LETTERS:** This quarterly magazine from the University of Missouri-Kansas City seeks writing that surprises and inspires. They want personal essays on any subject and fiction in these

categories: ethnic, experimental, humor, and mainstream. They pay $30 to $100 per published work.

14. **NINTH LETTER:** *Ninth Letter* is interested in publishing stories and essays that experiment with form, narrative, and nontraditional subject matter. They pay $25 per printed page, plus two contributor copies.

15. **OVERTIME:** *Overtime* is the only magazine I've ever seen that is dedicated specifically to working-class literature, a genre that has been a popular category among journals for years. They publish adventure, ethnic, experimental, historical, humor, mainstream, and slice-of-life short stories that are between 5,000 and 12,000 words, and they pay $35 to $50 per published work.

16. **THE RAG:** This genre magazine accepts gritty fantasy, horror, and science-fiction stories that may be up to 10,000 words long. They pay about $250 per published work, depending on the length of the story. *The Rag* is also looking for short fillers of 150 to 1,000 words.

17. **SEQUESTRUM:** This biweekly literary magazine acquires both essays and fiction. Essays may be general interest, humor, opinion, or personal experience; while fiction can be adventure, confession, experimental, literary, fantasy, horror, humor, mystery, science fiction, suspense, western, and slipstream. Submissions may not exceed 5,000 words, and they pay $10 to $15 per published story.

18. **THEMA:** *Thema* challenges writers to write a personal essay or short story with a specific theme in mind. Check *Thema*'s website for current and future themes. Categories accepted include adventure, ethnic, experimental, fantasy, historical, humor, mystery, religion, science fiction, and suspense. Submissions may be 300 to 6,000 words, and they pay $10 to $25 per published work.

19. **THE THREEPENNY REVIEW:** This quarterly magazine acquires both essays and short stories in any style. *The Threepenny Review* is known to have an experimental and adventurous attitude. Submissions may be 1,200 to 2,500 words, and they pay $400 per published work.

20. **VESTAL REVIEW:** *Vestal Review* is a magazine devoted specifically to flash fiction. All short stories must be between 50 and 500 words long. Styles accepted include: ethnic, fantasy, horror, humor, and mainstream. They pay three to ten cents per word.

As you can see, every magazine has a list of wants and needs. Some magazines are very specific, and others are more general. To make an authentic match to a magazine, make sure your word count and categories reflect the magazine's requirements.

ONLINE VS. PRINT PUBLICATIONS

Many literary journals have an online presence to accompany their print journal, sharing some content in print and other content online. *Tin House*, for example, features flash fiction weekly in their online market, "The Open Bar." Some magazines publish a few of their printed stories online to allow readers to sample what the journal has to offer in their current issue. Other journals are exclusively online.

These online only journals are becoming more common as magazine production and distribution costs increase. Online journals are relatively inexpensive to maintain, and issues can be formatted quickly, dramatically speeding up the process. Some online journals produce a new issue every single week.

There are some great benefits to being published in online journals. Faster production schedules mean shorter times between acceptance letters and actual publication of your work. Print journals can take up to a year before publishing your accepted work, while online journals usually publish your work within three months. Also, when you're published online, your work is archived with the magazine for eternity (or until the magazine closes its doors). That means that you can send the link to your story or essay to friends and family, add the link to your website, and share your work quickly via social media.

Online journals are less expensive to maintain, but that doesn't mean they're profitable. Like literary journals, online journals are usually a low-paying market. Many online journals don't offer anything for publication but exposure. Literary agents and book publishers read online journals as often as ones in print. That exposure is important, but a writer doesn't need constant exposure. Your other goals need attention, too.

Something to consider: Printed copies of magazines are still considered the pinnacle of prestige in literary magazines, especially as they become increasingly rare. Revisit your list of goals, and make sure you're getting what you want out of the bargain every time you send your work to editors.

WHERE TO FIND MAGAZINES LOOKING FOR WRITERS LIKE YOU

To make submission choices, you need to locate a batch of potential markets. The most widely used and well-known resource for finding places to send polished writing is *Writer's Market*. This paperback marketing reference has more than 3,500 listings of book publishers, consumer magazines, trade journals, writing contests, and literary agents. You can find *Writer's Market* at bookstores across the country. At about $30, this book is an indispensable resource. Fiction writers might also consider buying the *Novel & Short Story Writer's Market*. Every entry is a book publisher, magazine, agent, or contest interested in acquiring fiction.

Libraries and bookstores (and some grocery stores) have a magazine section, organized by category. Creative-writing opportunities are generally found in the "literary" section, but don't neglect the other magazines on the rack. There are hundreds of niche magazines looking for freelance writers, too. For writing opportunities, check the last page or two of each magazine. For example: *Psychology Today* has a section called "Two-Minute Memoir" in the back of their magazine. In these 1,500-word essays, the author writes about personal transformation (without any clinical or research background). Think about the topics in your work. Maybe that humorous story about your dog can find a home in *The Bark*. Perhaps a fitness magazine will be interested in your yoga-inspired essay.

Another great way to find markets is to pick up a short-story or essay collection. You'll find these housed with other books. Collections are groups of stories or essays all written by the same person. For the best research opportunity, select a collection where the voice or style of the pieces is similar to your own. Many of the included works are those that have been previously published in journals, which will be listed at the front of the book.

The Internet is another wonderful research tool. There are several online resources for finding creative-writing markets, including:

- **THE REVIEW REVIEW:** (www.thereviewreview.net) This is my favorite market resource for placing short stories and literary essays and not just because I spent two years on the editing team there (okay, I am a little biased). This magazine is dedicated to helping writers navigate the world of lit mags. *The Review Review* has a fantastic database of literary magazines and interviews with a plethora of editors. Each week there is a new "Publishing Tips" article, and founder Becky Tuch has one of the best free weekly newsletters in the industry. She had this to say about her publication:

  > I began *The Review Review* in 2008 in order to fill what I perceived to be a void in the literary landscape. Back then, there wasn't much detailed information about literary magazines. I wanted to create a forum that would provide writers with a deeper understanding of every journal, what kinds of stories, essays, and poetry they tend to favor, how carefully edited they are, what the magazine seems to be looking for, etc. I also wanted to open up a discussion surrounding lit mags. We hear all the time that no one reads these journals, that they are irrelevant, but they are so very important to writers! By creating a space for honest, engaged reviews, I hoped to create renewed engagement with lit mags overall, and to ensure their longevity.

- **WRITER'S DIGEST:** (www.writersdigest.com) This online companion to the print magazine has a terrific database of articles about the craft of writing and publishing opportunities. They are a resource for online classes as well. I subscribe to the print version of this magazine, too, because it is one of the most comprehensive industry resources around.

- **DUOTROPE:** (www.duotrope.com) This search engine for short story, essay, and article writers and poets contains information on every literary magazine in the country. You tell the website what you wrote (item, length, genre, etc), then decide how much you'd like to be paid and if you'd like to see all magazines or just those available in print. They will provide you with a list of magazines that meet your requirements and with links to each magazine. They also have a monthly list of anthology opportunities. Duotrope used to be a free service but now costs $5 per month.

- **BEYOND YOUR BLOG:** (www.beyondyourblog.com/opportunities-online) This is a fantastic resource for placing personal essays. Nonfiction opportunities are listed by category and are updated regularly.

- **NEWPAGES:** (www.newpages.com) NewPages posts news and information about lit mags, publishers, creative-writing programs, writing contests, and more.

- **FUNDS FOR WRITERS:** (www.fundsforwriters.com) At freelance writer Hope Clark's website, sign up for the free weekly newsletter and have new markets sent to your e-mail each week.

- **POETS & WRITERS:** (www.pw.org) The long-established and well-respected writer's magazine has a wonderful online version. They list anthology and magazine opportunities every month.

- **AEROGRAMME WRITERS' STUDIO:** (www.aerogrammestudio.com) This is a great weekly blog about local and international writing opportunities.

- **ASSOCIATION OF WRITERS & WRITING PROGRAMS:** (www.awpwriter.org) This community of writers and writing instructors has a yearly membership that includes access to contest information and calls for submissions from literary magazines around the country. AWP also hosts an annual conference where you can meet literary-magazine editors.

- **GOOGLE:** Search for more markets using keywords such as: *writing markets, essays, submission guidelines, call for submissions, freelance writing, dog stories, adventure stories,* etc.

ANOTHER GREAT MARKET: WRITING CONTESTS

There are hundreds of writing contests available each year, with prizes in cash or publication, and sometimes both. Contests can be a terrific way to get your writing noticed by editors and book publishers. Some are more prestigious than others, but all of them give you a chance to be read.

Contests are a great place to showcase your very best work. The competition is stiff, especially in the more well-known contests, so make sure your manuscript is polished and ready to be judged.

Nearly all contests ask for an entry fee. It isn't unheard of to spend up to $20 for entry to a very distinguished literary competition, although many fees are lower. Make sure you feel the fee you pay is equitable for the prize they're offering. Let your personal writing goals lead you.

You can find contest listings in many of the same places you find magazine listings, including *Writer's Market* and *Poets & Writers*. You can also do a quick Google search by contest name or search for "writing contests."

Most contests will publish the winning entries. Read the winning entries from previous years to best understand what the contest is looking for in submissions. Here are a few reputable writing contests you might consider (contest information was accurate at the time of this book's original publication):

Essay Writing Contests

1. **NEW LETTERS PRIZE FOR NONFICTION:** This contest is offered annually to discover and reward emerging writers. Send unpublished

essays of up to 8,000 words. First place: $1,500 and publication, sponsored by the literary magazine *New Letters*.

2. **HUNGER MOUNTAIN CREATIVE NONFICTION PRIZE:** This annual contest rewards the best writing in creative nonfiction. Send unpublished essays of up to 10,000 words. First place: $1,000 and publication in *Hunger Mountain*.

3. **LITERAL LATTÉ ESSAY AWARD:** This contest is open to any writer, and works may be on any topic. All essays must be unpublished and not exceed 10,000 words. First place: $1,000; second place: $300; third place: $200.

4. **LINDA JOY MYERS MEMOIR VIGNETTE PRIZE:** This contest is part of the Soul-Making Keats Literary Competition and is open annually to any writer. Send one entry of up to 1,500 words. Previously published material is accepted. First place: $100; second place: $50; third place: $25.

5. **DIAGRAM ESSAY CONTEST:** Sponsored by the Department of English at the University of Arizona, writers may enter essays of up to 10,000 words. First place: $1,000 and publication.

6. **ANNIE DILLARD AWARD FOR CREATIVE NONFICTION:** Sponsored by *Bellingham Review*, it is offered annually for unpublished essays on any subject and in any style. First place: $1,000 and publication, plus copies of the issue where their essay appears.

7. **JOHN GUYON LITERARY NONFICTION PRIZE:** Sponsored by *Crab Orchard Review*, this annual award is for unpublished creative nonfiction. Essays of up to 6,500 words are eligible. First place: $1,250 and publication.

8. **GAIL WILSON KENNA CREATIVE NONFICTION PRIZE:** Sponsored by the Soul-Making Keats Literary Competition, creative nonfiction of up to 3,000 words is eligible. First place: $100; second place: $50; third place: $25.

9. **MONTANA PRIZE IN CREATIVE NONFICTION:** Sponsored by *Cut-Bank*, this contest accepts one creative nonfiction essay of up to thirty-five pages per participant. Prize: $500 and a feature in *CutBank*.

10. **WRITER'S DIGEST ANNUAL WRITING COMPETITION:** Open to any writer, essays of up to 2,000 words are eligible. Grand Prize: $5,000, publication, paid admission to the *Writer's Digest* Annual Conference, and other prizes; first place: $1,000.

Short Story Contests

1. **BOULEVARD SHORT FICTION CONTEST FOR EMERGING WRITERS:** Open to any writer who hasn't yet published a book of fiction (novel or short-story collection), participants may send stories of up to 8,000 words. First place: $1,500 and publication in *Boulevard*.
2. **CHARITON REVIEW SHORT FICTION PRIZE:** This is an annual award for the best, unpublished short fiction on any theme. Writers may send stories of up to 5,000 words. First place: $500 and publication in *Chariton Review*.
3. **BELLEVUE LITERARY REVIEW GOLDENBERG PRIZE FOR FICTION:** The *BLR* awards outstanding writing related to the themes of health, healing, illness, the mind, and the body. Writers may send stories of up to 5,000 words. First place: $1,000 and publication in *Bellevue Literary Review*.
4. **DEADLY QUILL SHORT STORY WRITING CONTEST:** Stories that echo *The Twilight Zone*, Alfred Hitchcock, and *The Outer Limits* are the focus of this competition. First place: $250; second place: $200; third place: $150.
5. **THE GHOST STORY SUPERNATURAL FICTION AWARD:** Submissions may or may not include ghosts. Any paranormal or supernatural theme is welcome, as well as magical realism. The contest accepts stories that are between 1,500 words and 10,000 words. First place: $1,000 and publication in *The Ghost Story*.
6. **GIVAL PRESS SHORT STORY AWARD:** This press acquires novels and short-story collections, making it a great place to get your fiction noticed. To enter the contest, send unpublished short stories that are between 5,000 and 15,000 words. First place: $1,000 and publication on the Gival Press website and in an upcoming anthology.

Writing & Selling Short Stories & Personal Essays

7. **GLIMMER TRAIN'S SHORT STORY AWARD FOR NEW WRITERS:** This contest is open to any writer whose fiction hasn't appeared in a nationally distributed magazine, and participants may send fiction that is no more than 12,000 words. First place: $2,500 and publication; second place: $500; third place: $300.

8. **WILDA HEARNE FLASH FICTION CONTEST:** Sponsored by Southeast Missouri State University Press, this competition is open to any writer and accepts unpublished stories of up to 500 words. First place: $500 and publication in *Big Muddy: A Journal of the Mississippi River Valley*.

9. **ZOETROPE: ALL STORY SHORT STORY CONTEST:** Sponsored by *Zoetrope: All Story*, submissions may be up to 7,000 words in length. First place: $1,000 and publication on the website; second place: $500; third place: $250.

10. **WRITER'S DIGEST ANNUAL WRITING COMPETITION:** Open to both genre and literary short stories, writers may send fiction of up to 4,000 words. Grand Prize: $5,000, publication, paid admission to the *Writer's Digest* Annual Conference, and other prizes; first place: $1,000.

SUBMISSION GUIDELINES

Every potential magazine has guidelines for writers that identify what kind of material they accept. These are called submission guidelines or writers' guidelines. These guidelines tell you what you need to know about submitting to their magazine, including:

1. the types of writing they acquire (ex: essay, creative nonfiction, short story, flash fiction)
2. the length of writing they accept
3. whether or not they are currently open to submissions
4. their general submission window (September through December, for instance)
5. what they offer as payment (ex: money, free subscription to magazine, contributor copies, exposure)

6. how many stories or essays you can submit at one time (multiple submissions)
7. whether it's okay for you to send the same story to another magazine at the same time (simultaneous submissions)
8. how they accept work (ex: e-mail, Submittable, snail mail)
9. whether they charge a reading fee

Many magazines go even further into detail and include information about styles they prefer, what they don't want to see in submissions, and exactly how they'd like you to format your work. Some magazines have themed issues that they'll discuss in the guidelines.

You can find writers' guidelines at a magazine's website, but it might not be easy to locate. If you don't see a link to submission information on the front page, find the contact page or a "frequently asked questions" section. If you can't find what you're looking for there, try a quick Google search. Something like "*The Sunlight Press* magazine submissions."

If, after all of that, you still can't find the writers' guidelines for a magazine, that's no accident. Magazines that don't have public writers' guidelines are not seeking freelance submissions. Many larger magazines have a stable of freelance writers they work with exclusively. If you'd like to be published in one of the magazines with an exclusive staff, send a formal business letter to the main editor, asking about opportunities at the magazine.

Multiple and Simultaneous Submissions

The term "multiple submissions" refers to a batch of stories or essays that you send to one editor all at the same time. In the writers' guidelines, editors who accept multiple submissions will state so, and it's great when they do. It increases your chances of placing at least one of the pieces that you send. Multiple submissions are most common when submitting flash fiction.

The term "simultaneous submissions" refers to when you send the exact same story or essay to multiple magazines at the same time. It's one of the most important things to decipher in the writers' guidelines. Most journals expect that you'll send your work to many editors at a time, but some magazines request an exclusive read of your work. Editors who request an exclusive are generally quick to reply to queries, out of respect to the writer, but some are big-name magazines with large backlogs of submissions (*The Sun*, for instance). When this is the case, the editors can't get back to you with an answer for several months.

A journal who wants an exclusive read of your work will say so by telling you "no simultaneous submissions" somewhere in the guidelines or "no sim subs" (for short). Magazines that accept simultaneous submissions will say so in the guidelines with a disclaimer that usually reads: "Simultaneous submissions are okay, but please let us know if your story is picked up by another journal."

That last part is important, "… please let us know if your story is picked up by another journal." Your responsibility as a writer sending out simultaneous submissions is to keep potential editors informed about the status of your work. When your work is accepted, let the other journals know that your work is no longer available. This is common courtesy. It is customary to send this notice within twenty-four hours of accepting a contract.

Submission Fees

Some literary and genre magazines will charge you a reading fee when you submit your writing. This happens at magazines that pay and also at magazines that don't. This practice is relatively new to our industry. It looks like it might be here to stay, so you need to be aware of the trend. To make the best submission choices, decide how you feel about this financial investment, and submit work according to your opinion.

Some important things to note:

1. This fee is nonrefundable, even if you withdraw your submission.
2. The fee is charged to your credit card at the time of submission.
3. Most magazines that charge a reading fee have a short window each year where you can submit your work for free.
4. This fee does not make any magazine rich (or even profitable).

Magazines that charge reading fees say they do so because it helps offset their production costs or it helps reduce their submissions to a manageable number. Reading fees for short stories and essays run from $1–5 per submission, but some are as high as $22 or more.

Usually writers are able to submit up to three pieces of flash fiction as one submission, making the fee cover a bit more ground when writing very short pieces. Even so, submission fees can add up quickly for a freelance writer. At $3 per submission, you could spend $30 or more on reading fees before ever getting an acceptance letter. And then, if all you receive as payment is exposure, you're in the red, financially. And that's just for one story. Imagine writing a terrific new story every month.

Luckily you have plenty of choices when it comes to submitting short writing. Many magazines don't charge reading fees, and most of those that do offer you a large enough dose of exposure to make it worth your while. It's up to you to decide when the cost of submitting is worth the reward and how many times you can afford to submit to magazines that charge you.

Back when I first started submitting essays and stories, submissions were accomplished by regular mail. I had to buy books and books of stamps and stacks of envelopes in legal and letter sizes. A financial investment was part of the deal, so I'm not opposed to spending some money on submissions. It feels familiar, but I am opposed to magazines that make a profit from writers by submission fees. This is a rare thing since most literary magazines don't make a profit at all, but I'm careful about submitting for a fee. I investigate each submission thoroughly and only submit to those magazines I feel comfortable with as partners. Not everybody makes the cut. If the fee is more than a few dollars, I usually submit elsewhere.

To keep from going broke, I allow myself a yearly submission budget. I have to deduct from that budget every time I send work to a magazine that charges reading fees, and the practice makes me very selective. It might work for you as well. There is some good news: No matter how many fee-charging magazines you send your work to in a year, all submission fees can be written off your taxes—along with your postage costs.

FIND THE RIGHT MATCH

To match your work to a magazine, start by familiarizing yourself with their needs. Do they accept short stories and essays or *just* essays? Does your word count fit their magazine? If a magazine accepts short stories between 1,000 and 7,000 words and you've written a 3,000-word short story, you have the potential for a match.

Next, check their submission window. Are they currently open to submissions? And how about the pay? Does the remuneration match your current writing goals?

And what about your categories? Are the editors looking for humorous essays? Travel stories? Mysteries? Narrative poems? Sometimes editors will list very specific items they are looking for, and sometimes a magazine will just advise you to send your best work.

If the magazine you've selected does have more information to share, read it thoroughly. If the magazine doesn't accept erotica or violence, don't send them erotic or violent stories. If the editors say they're looking for pieces with a positive message, respect that, too. When editors tell you what they want, listen. Only submit stories and essays that meet their editorial tastes.

Lastly, compare your tone and voice to those in the works within the magazine. Sometimes you'll be able to read a story or two online; other times you'll need to get your hands on a physical copy of the magazine.

Some magazines offer a "sample copy" to potential contributors at a discounted price. If that's the case, you'll read about it in the writers' guidelines. It can be expensive to spend $11 to $14 per magazine, so take any discount you can find. Buy a few, and then trade magazines with your writer friends.

My favorite frugal way to read literary magazines is to visit your local MFA program, even if you aren't a student. Find one where they run a literary magazine in-house. These programs have yearly subscriptions to several other literary magazines, and, if you ask nicely, they'll usually let you read some.

SENDING TO CONTESTS AND MAGAZINES AT THE SAME TIME

Sometimes you see a writing contest and know that you've written a piece that's perfect for it, but you've already sent that piece out to a magazine or two. However, you still might be able to play in both places at the same time. Do some research. Check the writers' guidelines where you've already submitted your work. If they accept simultaneous submissions, you're fine.

Next, read the contest details carefully. If they also accept simultaneous submissions, then you can send them your story. Also, if there isn't publication offered as part of the contest prize, you can send them your story since you won't be granting any rights to your work. If the contest doesn't mention anything about simultaneous submissions (many don't), then you'll need to send the contest editor a quick note and ask them about their current policy.

YOUR TURN: FIND POTENTIAL MARKETS FOR YOUR WORK

Now you're ready to decide exactly where to send your finished short stories and essays. You know how to find potential magazines, so let's start there. Let's say you decide to go online to *The Review Review* first. You get to the website's main page and find the "magazines" tab at the top. You click on that and land at the submission database.

From here, all you need to do is click on the magazine names to be taken directly to their writers' guidelines. Or, if you'd like to filter things according to your specific publishing needs, fill out the section on the right side of the screen. You'll get to decide if you want to see magazines that publish online or in print, what kind of payment you're interested in, and whether or not you're willing to pay a reading fee. Have your list of categories nearby. Refer back to it every time you read the writers' guidelines. When you find a match, write it down, and look for another.

....

"One of the best ways to find the right magazines for your writing is to get to know the contributors lists in various journals. For instance, if you know that you enjoy reading a particular magazine and feel that magazine suits your own aesthetic, read the bios of the writers published there. Which other magazines have those writers published in? Track down those other journals, and familiarize yourself with those. Be open-minded, and remain curious. Eventually, you will begin to create a kind of mental map of the literary landscape. If you know about fifteen to twenty magazines ... that publish work you like and where you think your work would be a good fit, then you are well ahead of the game."

—BECKY TUCH

....

As you study potential magazines and newspapers, you can create a personalized resource file or spreadsheet—something that will make your job easier next time you're looking through magazines. On a separate sheet of paper, list any markets that look interesting to you, even if you don't have something to send them yet. Next time you have a polished piece in your hands, you can refer to your markets list instead of working from scratch. You might want to transfer your list to a computer file for safe keeping or organize your markets in a binder with tabs (I use a binder with tabs so that I can rip pages out of writing magazines and tuck them inside). Whatever method you choose, make sure your resource file is easy to access and update.

Joan, Samantha, and Hershel checked the magazines listed in this book for inspiration before going online. Joan has decided she'll send a story each to *The Sun* and *Ellipsis* since they are well-known literary journals. Samantha chose *Hunger Mountain* and *New Letters* for her travel and humor essays. Hershel liked the guidelines from *Hunger Mountain*, too, so he'll send a story there and submit another story to *Apex*. Check that list of magazines, and see if any fit the aesthetic of your polished work.

Keep hunting down markets that perfectly match your writing until you have five solid leads. When you're done, set things aside and get ready to craft a letter to the editors.

16

COVER LETTERS

A cover letter (sometimes called a query) is an introduction to the writing project you'd like to submit. The introduction for short stories and essays is brief, just a few sentences in a one-page business letter.

There are four main parts to a cover letter. They can be broken down like this:

1. "Hello"
2. "Here's What I'm Sending"
3. "Here's Who I Am"
4. "Thank You"

You want to begin your cover letter with a personalized greeting. Find the name of the appropriate editor, and fill that in at the top. The key to writing an effective cover letter is professionalism. Be formal here.

Example: *Dear Ms. Johnson,*

Next, introduce your work in the first paragraph. Include the title and word count. Editors don't need to know the content of your essay or story, but you can add a line about it *if you'd like*. It's more important to tell the editor why you're submitting to their specific magazine. Maybe you liked a certain piece from last month's issue, or maybe you have a friend who has already been published there. Use sincerity only; if you don't have any reason for selecting this magazine beyond feeling like your work is a match, that's fine. You can mention that, too.

Your writing credentials belong in the middle paragraph. Before you have publishing credits to talk about, use this paragraph to mention any writing groups you're part of, an MFA, or writing classes. You could also tell the editor your reason for writing the piece. For example, *This story was inspired by the summer I worked as a hot dog vendor in New York.* After you have been published, list your publishing credits instead. As your success mounts, pick the best three credits to list.

The last paragraph is where you should thank the editor for her time and let her know you are looking forward to hearing from her. This is also the place where you might refer to any specific directions you read in the writers' guidelines. For instance, if the editor has asked that you attach a copy of the manuscript rather than put it in the body of the e-mail, you can acknowledge that you've followed that direction with a quick sentence like, *I have attached the completed essay for your review.*

The don'ts:

- Never mention who has previously rejected the piece.
- Do not request advice or comments.
- Do not talk about how thrilling it would be to be published.
- Do not discuss payment.

This is a business letter, not a fan letter. You just want to politely introduce yourself and your project. Make it short and sweet. Leave an editor nodding her head, ready to read your submission.

Once you create a custom cover letter for a specific piece of your creative writing, you can send that same letter to as many editors as it takes to find your work a good home—just remember to change the editor's name and the magazine information before you send it out the door.

WHICH EDITOR SHOULD I CONTACT?

Magazine editors have many titles in this business, including managing editor, senior editor, manuscript editor, assistant editor—the list goes on and on. Typically there's one main editor in charge, the editor-in-chief, who coordinates a group of other editors (ex: the fiction editor, the poetry editor, the nonfiction editor). You want to send your cover letters to the most appropriate editor for your piece of writing, but with all of those job titles available, sometimes it's difficult to figure that out. You'll find the list of editors in a magazine's masthead. If you're at a magazine's website, you might find the masthead in its own tab or you might look for a section titled "About Us." Short stories should be directed to the fiction editor—when there is a fiction editor—and essays should be directed to the nonfiction editor, but some magazines don't have those two titles listed. When that's the case, send your query letter to the editor-in-chief or managing editor of that magazine. Both of these titles describe the main editor. This editor will know who is available to read your submission and will direct your submission to the right person. If you don't see editor-in-chief or managing editor listed, look to the top of the masthead and send your query to that editor. If you can't find the main editor's name at all (it happens a lot), begin your letter with "Dear Editors."

ONE MORE THING TO WRITE: THE THIRD-PERSON BIO

A third-person biography is different from the middle paragraph of your cover letter. This bio is the few lines of information about you that will be published with your work in the magazine. It is written, as indicated, in third person (with *he/she/they* pronouns).

Often this bio is printed at the bottom of your story or essay next to your name, but sometimes contributors are listed in the back of a journal. Many magazines ask you to send them a third-person bio along with your submission package so they don't have to follow up later. Typically this bio is 50 words or less, but some magazines allow up to 100 words.

To write your own third-person bio, think about what you'd like readers to know. You can express anything you'd like in this bio; there are no set rules. Some writers like to list a few places they've been published; some list their relevant writing credentials, and others prefer to express their personalities. All of these ideas are appropriate.

I like to tailor mine toward the audience of the magazine. If it's a quirky mag, I might use humor in my bio. For literary magazines, I tend to list publications and maybe add some awards I've received. In regional magazines, I like to mention where I live or what hobbies I enjoy. Add your website if you have one, and add the titles of books that you've published. Let people find you! Below are some of my own third-person bios:

> Windy Lynn Harris (www.windylynnharris.com) has written short stories and personal essays that have appeared in *The Literary Review*, *Pithead Chapel*, and *Literary Mama*, among many other journals. She has been the recipient of fellowships at The Maribar Writers Colony and Dorland Mountain Arts Colony. She is working on her first novel.

> Windy Lynn Harris is from Phoenix, AZ. She writes under the watchful eye of Paragraph, her faithful dog. When she's not at her desk, you'll find Windy near the bar at Changing Hands Bookstore (especially on pie day) or meandering up one of the local mountains in search of petroglyphs. You can find out more about Windy and her writing at www.windylynnharris.com.

> Windy Lynn Harris (www.windylynnharris.com) is the author of *Writing & Selling Short Stories & Personal Essays: The Essential Guide to Getting Your Work Published*. She is also the founder of Market Coaching for Creative Writers, a mentorship program that teaches writers how to get their short stories, essays, and poems published in magazines. She is a frequent speaker at literary events.

FORMATTING THE COVER LETTER

Some of your cover letters will be sent digitally to editors, while others will be sent by post (snail mail, as we call it). In either situation, you'll need to format your cover letter to these industry standards:

1. Use twelve-point font and Times New Roman or Courier (no fancy script).
2. Use block-paragraph format (single-space paragraphs with an extra space between paragraphs—no indents).
3. Use 1 to 1-½" margins all around.

4. Address your letter to the proper editor, and spell the name correctly (double-check—is it *Mr.* Smith or *Ms.* Smith?) E-mailed submissions do not need this letterhead.

When you send your cover letter by snail mail, you need to do a few additional things:

1. At the top-left corner, add your name, address, e-mail address, website (if you have one), and phone number. These items are single-spaced.
2. Add the date of your submission below the header.
3. Add the magazine's contact information below the date.
4. Leave three extra lines after your closing so that you have room to sign your name.
5. Tell the editor what you've sent in a short enclosure line (*Encl: manuscript and SASE*). SASE stands for self-addressed stamped envelope. We'll get to that later, but for now, know that when you send submissions by post that you must include a stamped envelope for her reply.

Cover Letter Examples

A cover letter sent by e-mail:

> Dear Ms. Bailey:
>
> I'm submitting my 100-word flash fiction story, "Everyone Says So," for your consideration. I am sending you this story because I read in your writers' guidelines that you're looking for writing that bridges the gap between dream and reality.
>
> My work has been published in *The Literary Review*, *34thParallel*, and *Poor Mojo's Almanac(k)*, among many other journals.
>
> Thank you for your time. I look forward to hearing from you.
>
> Sincerely,
> Fabulous Writer

An e-mail cover letter sent from a new writer:

Dear Mr. Daniels:

Please consider the following 700-word short story, "Ferris Wheel," for your publication.

This story is based on my own memories of growing up in a small resort town. I think it would fit well alongside the other nostalgic pieces you print in *American Short Fiction*.

Thank you for your time and for considering "Ferris Wheel." I have attached the completed manuscript, per your request.

Sincerely,
Fabulous Writer

A cover letter sent by snail mail:

Fabulous Writer
Your address here
And here
Your e-mail
Your website
Your phone number

December 3, 2018

Jane Doe, Editor

Blue Collar Review
P.O. Box 11417
Norfolk, VA 23517

Dear Ms. Doe:

I am sending you my 552-word essay, "Me and I Pack a Suitcase," for consideration in *Blue Collar Review*. As you will see in this humorous piece, packing for a trip is hard enough without your subconscious getting in the way.

In addition to placing in three national humor-writing contests, my work has been published recently in *Raising Arizona Kids* magazine, *Sasee*, and *Mom Writer's Literary Magazine*.

Thank you for your time and for considering "Me and I Pack a Suitcase." I look forward to hearing from you.

Sincerely,
Fabulous Writer

Encl: Manuscript and SASE

(Remember: After printing your cover letter, be sure to sign it.)

THE PITCH LETTER (SELLING ARTICLES)

If you're interested in selling articles, the following is a brief overview of what you need to know about approaching editors. Writers with an expertise or interest in any subject can write articles. I write articles for the writing community these days, but there was a time in the past when I pitched "how-to" articles in the parenting market.

Writing articles can be a great way to add bylines to your résumé. Some writers sell articles as a way of generating (extra) income. Others write articles to promote their book projects. Sometimes a writer working on a novel or a memoir does research that turns out to be interesting enough to share in his books as well as in an article. If you have a hobby or work in an industry where you've become an expert in something, why not share what you know with the world?

Articles are sold differently than short stories and essays. Earlier in this book, we talked about the difference between essays and articles. Let's review that now. Articles are factual pieces of writing on a topic. They are written in third person with an informational tone.

You don't write an article before you sell it (though you could). Instead, you come up with a great idea for an article and pitch it to an editor. If she likes your idea, she'll give you a contract for the article, and then you will write it.

A pitch letter is the kind of query you'll use to entice that nonfiction editor. Pitch letters are usually just called "query letters."

To pitch articles effectively, you need to match your idea with the right magazine. There are thousands of commercial and trade magazines publishing all kinds of articles. You'll find great opportunities in some of the same places you'll find essay and story markets, especially *Writer's Market, Writer's Digest,* and Duotrope.

Read a copy of a magazine to see if your article idea fits their vibe. Really study it. Look at who the magazine's advertising is geared toward. Would your article idea appeal to those same people? Also, check the magazine's website for a media kit. The media kit will give you demographic information about the people who read the magazine.

All magazines that work with freelance writers will have writers' guidelines available to you online. Read the guidelines carefully, and craft your pitch accordingly. For example: If the editor is looking for articles between 800 and 2,000 words, make sure you pitch something in that range.

Journals require you to know your topic well. Emphasize your expertise on a subject in your pitch. You may need to do a lot of research for your article, and that's fine. You might consider interviewing other experts for your article to increase the expertise factor.

What Goes Into a Pitch Letter?

The pitch letter for an article is short and formal, containing your idea in specific terms. A pitch letter has the same basic format as other cover letters: block-style body with a space between paragraphs. Search the masthead for the appropriate editor to query. The big difference between this type of letter and the one you'll write for short stories and essays is in the body. Instead of a general *Hi, this is my finished piece* letter, the pitch letter is a sales tool. You're putting your idea in front of an editor and hoping he'll buy it for the magazine.

First, you need a hook. A great opening will entice the editor to read your whole idea. It might even become the title of your piece. Sum up your idea in one sentence.

Next, you need to explain—in one paragraph—what the focus of the article will be. Let the editor know if the article will inform, educate, inspire, and/or entertain.

The next paragraph is where you add specifics. Tell the editor your proposed word count and where you think it will fit in the magazine. Perhaps you'll interview someone or combine your article with photos. Include that here.

Last, give your qualifications for writing the article. This is the place to tell the editor about your prior writing credits. The most important thing here is to demonstrate that you are the perfect person to write this article. This means that your prior writing credits are great, and you should mention them (especially if they support your authority on the subject). Don't worry if your credits are in a different area of writing or if you don't have any bylines yet. Convince the editor that you're an expert *by experience*. If you're writing an article about competitive running and you've entered races across the country, say that in your pitch letter. It will prove your credibility.

Example of a Pitch Letter

Editor's name
Publication name
Editor's address

Dear Editor (insert real name),

There are thirty-two no-kill pet shelters in the state of Arizona, but only one that provides massage therapy for incoming animals—Labor Of Love Rescue.

Located in the heart of downtown Phoenix, Labor Of Love Rescue has spent the past decade providing a safe refuge for severely neglected and abused animals. Along the way, they have earned a reputation for rehabilitating dogs and cats that society had given up on. Donna McGuire, a certified massage therapist, leads the inspiring team of volunteers.

I propose writing a piece on Labor Of Love Rescue for your Making a Difference department. After years of reading this heartening column, I believe your readership would appreciate the unique mission at Labor Of Love Rescue. Donna McGuire has already agreed to let me interview her and has offered access to their facilities for additional information.

The piece would run about 800–1,000 words and would include photographs. I am one of the many people who have adopted a wonderful pet from Labor Of Love Rescue. I am also a member of PETA.

Thank you for your consideration of this article. I hope to hear from you soon.

Sincerely,
Your Name,
Address
Your e-mail, phone #

SOME TOPICS TO WRITE ABOUT & WHERE TO QUERY

ANIMALS: Birding World, Catster, Equine Journal
ART AND ARCHITECTURE: Art Papers, Metropolis, Modernism
ASSOCIATIONS: AAA Living, American Educator, Kiwanis
ASTROLOGY AND NEW AGE: Fate Magazine, Whole Life Times, Witches & Pagans
AUTOMOTIVE: Autoweek, Rider, RoadKing
AVIATION: The Autopilot, Flying, Pipers Magazine
BUSINESS AND FINANCE: Business Traveler, Fortune, Profit
CAREER, COLLEGE, AND ALUMNI: Career Options, Harvard Magazine, Woman Engineer
CHILD CARE AND PARENTAL GUIDANCE: Family Fun, Homeschooling Today, Today's Parent
CONTEMPORARY CULTURE: Broken Pencil, Commentary, The Futurist
DISABILITIES: Abilities, Arthritis Today, Kaleidoscope
ENTERTAINMENT: Flick, In Touch Weekly, Sound & Vision
ETHNIC AND MINORITY: AIM Magazine, Filipinas, Italian America
FOOD AND DRINK: Draft, Vegetarian Journal, Wine Spectator
GAMES AND PUZZLES: Chess Life, Games, Poker Pro
GAY AND LESBIAN: The Advocate, Echo, Instinct
GENERAL INTEREST: National Geographic, Parade, Reader's Digest
HEALTH AND FITNESS: Climbing, Men's Health, Shape
HISTORY: Civil War Times, History Magazine, Wild West
HOBBY AND CRAFT: Antique Trader, Classic Toy Trains, Kitplanes
HOME AND GARDEN: Better Homes and Gardens, Country Living, This Old House
JUVENILE: Boys' Life, Highlights, Ladybug
MILITARY: Air Force Times, Proceedings, Soldier Of Fortune

MUSIC: *Bluegrass Unlimited, Chamber Music, Symphony*
NATURE AND ECOLOGY: *Birdwatching, Ocean, Outdoor America*
POLITICS: *Church & State, The Progressive, The Progressive Populist*
RELIGION: *America, Catholic Digest, Guideposts*
RETIREMENT: *AARP The Magazine, Mature Living, Christian Living in the Mature Years*
RURAL: *Farm & Ranch Living, Hobby Farms, Range*
SCIENCE: *Ad Astra, American Archaeology, Scientific American*
SPORTS: *Bowhunter, Adventure Cyclist, Sailing World*
TEEN AND YOUNG ADULT: *Cicada, Listen, Seventeen*
TRAVEL: *Camping Today, MotorHome, Pathfinders Travel*
WOMEN'S: *Complete Woman, Country Woman, Family Circle*

YOUR TURN: WRITE A COVER LETTER

It's time to try your hand at writing a cover letter. Select one of your polished pieces and the list of magazines you plan to approach. Begin by finding the editor's name—hunt through the masthead, and direct your cover letter to the most appropriate person. Introduce your writing in the first paragraph, and put your credentials in the middle paragraph. Then wrap up your short letter with a word of thanks.

Check the writers' guidelines again. Did the editor ask you to include a third-person bio? If so, create a short bio and slip it into the space where your credentials would go. Preface the bio with the phrase "My third-person bio."

If your cover letter will be sent via snail mail, be sure to add the additional contact information and leave a big space after your closing so that you can sign it once you've printed the page.

Here's what our friends Joan, Samantha, and Hershel came up with. This first example is from Joan, who will be submitting one of her essays to *Ellipsis*. She has a small connection to Westminster College, where the magazine is headquartered, so she's said something about that in her cover letter. There were several editors listed on the *Ellipsis* website. Joan decided to address her cover letter to the current editor-in-chief: Alaa Al-Barkawi. The writers' guidelines also stated that her cover letter should include her address, telephone number, and e-mail address, even though she'll be submitting her manuscript electronically. She's added that information below her salutation.

Dear Mr. Al-Barkawi:

I'm submitting a 2,500-word essay, "Kayaking My Way Back Home," for your consideration. My father was an administrator at Westminster College for three years during my childhood. I can still picture the white bark of the birch trees on High Hill.

I am a member of the Alabama Writers' Group and a lifelong reader.

Thank you for your time. I look forward to hearing from you.

Sincerely,
Joan Holloway
5555 State Ave.
Phoenix, AZ 85331
(555) 555-5555
joan@joanthewriter.com

This next example is from Samantha. Samantha plans to submit one of her essays to *Hunger Mountain*. She was able to identify the prose editor, Jedediah Berry, so she's decided to direct her letter to him. She doesn't have a reason for submitting her essay to *Hunger Mountain* beyond the fact that her essay feels like an authentic match, so she's expressed that in the first paragraph. The magazine has asked for a third-person bio, which she included in the second paragraph. The editors have requested all submissions be sent by e-mail with an attached manuscript, which Samantha has acknowledged in the last line.

Dear Mr. Berry:

Please consider the following 800-word essay, "Think Like A Dog; Travel Like A Cat," for publication in *Hunger Mountain*. I think it would be a good fit with the other humor and travel pieces you print.

My third-person bio: Samantha Beet is an an avid traveler who hates luggage. She has an MFA from Sarah Lawrence College where she volunteers as a mentor during the summer program. She is working on her first book, a memoir about her teenage years in Madagascar. You can visit Samantha online at www.samanthabeettravels.com.

Thank you for your time and for considering "Think Like A Dog; Travel Like A Cat." I have attached the completed manuscript, per your request.

Sincerely,
Samantha Beet

This one is from Hershel, who plans to send one of his stories to *Apex*. He'd like to see his work in a print magazine, and *Apex* is a beautiful, well-respected option. Luckily, it's also the perfect fit for one of his stories. The *Apex* writers' guidelines state that they do not accept simultaneous submissions, so he's decided to add a line to his cover letter that shows his acknowledgement of this. He doesn't mind giving *Apex* an exclusive read because the writers' guidelines also said that they respond to all submissions within thirty days. He's fine with that length of wait if it means he might land among the pages of *Apex*.

Dear Mr. Sizemore:

I am sending you an 1800-word story, "It's About the Girl," for consideration in *Apex*. I enjoy the stories I read in your magazine. "Waste," by Mary Elizabeth Burroughs, was a recent favorite.

I'm a prolific writer, working on my first short-story collection. My story "The Way He Walks" earned second place in the Hudson Valley Writer's Contest last fall.

This is an exclusive submission. Thank you for your time and for considering "It's About the Girl." I look forward to hearing from you soon.

Sincerely,
Hershel B. Langdon

FORMATTING YOUR MANUSCRIPT

Before sending your story or essay out the door, you'll need to properly format your work. Formatting includes setting your title where it belongs, adding a header, and making sure that your spacing is properly executed throughout. In any business, there is a right and wrong way to do things. I'll show you the freelance-writing industry standard for short creative writing.

Editors are busy people with plenty of short pieces stacked on their desks. Many writers get their work tossed into the automatic rejection pile without ever being read because their manuscript lacks a professional touch. Nobody knows for certain how many good stories and essays get passed over due to poor formatting, but I do know this: Proper formatting makes you look like a pro, someone who knows what they are doing. This, in turn, instills confidence in an editor about the actual story or essay itself. You can increase your chances of publication by following standard manuscript-formatting guidelines each time you send out your work.

....

"Incorrect formatting makes my job as an editor much more difficult. I will still peruse the submission for quality—the prose

and the point is more important than the format, of course—but format can make a submission look amateurish, which makes me balk. The piece has to be extraordinary for me to consider it a real contender for publication. Then, when it comes time to upload files digitally, incorrect formatting can cost me not mere hours but days, when enough submissions flood in incorrectly. I spend more time fixing stupid errors (and pulling out my hair with frustration) than concentrating on putting out quality work."

—SAVANNAH THORNE

GETTING STARTED

First, the basics:

1. Print manuscripts on 8-½" x 11", white paper (use only one side of the paper).
2. Use 1 to 1-½" margins all around.
3. Use twelve-point standard typeface: Times New Roman or Courier (or something similar).
4. There should be no end-of-the-line hyphenated words or justified right margins.
5. Double-space the entire manuscript.
6. Indent paragraphs five spaces (this is the preset on your "tab" button).
7. There should be no additional spacing between paragraphs.

Next, add identifying information, your byline, and the header:

8. Type your name, address, phone number, and e-mail address in the upper-left corner, single-spaced. In the upper-right corner, type the word count. You can round the word count up to the nearest hundred or the nearest ten in short pieces if you'd like. If you're writing under a pen name, place your real name (the person you want the check made out to) in the top-left corner on the first page.

Use your pen name as your byline underneath the title. It's always a good idea to mention in your query letter that you use a pen name.

9. Drop down about halfway on the first page, and center your title. Your byline goes beneath it. These are double-spaced.

10. On page two (and subsequent pages), add a header that includes your title and last name.

11. Be sure to double-check your page numbers and headers. They need to be in the same font as the rest of your manuscript. It won't happen automatically unless your program is preset to those specifications.

How to Create a Header

On page two of your manuscript, hover your cursor about one inch from the top to reveal the header bar. Type your title (or a key word from your title if it is very long) in the header bar, add a dash, and type your last name. Then add one more dash, two spaces, and your number (this extra space allows for double-digit page numbers).

Align your header text to the right. This allows the header to be in place without interrupting the flow of the prose as it is being read.

Make sure your header doesn't begin until the second page of your manuscript. This will leave page one clean and pretty. You might need to visit the headers and footers section of your word-processing program and mark the box that says (or says something similar to), "Hide on first page of section." The second page's text should begin three or four spaces below the header.

In the body of your work, save any italics, boldface, and words typed in all capital letters for times when you—artistically—want to emphasize something. Don't use them unless you really need to. Ask yourself, *Do I really need to use them?*

A caveat: Industry format standards were put in place to make your manuscript easy to read by those overworked editor eyes, but don't be too rigid on the small stuff. If you like your page numbers in a different spot—that's fine. Put them in a different spot. Want to capitalize your title? Do it. Just make sure the result is a manuscript that looks clean and professional.

One Space, Not Two

Should you use one space or two after closing a sentence with punctuation?

The answer: one space.

You only need to use one space after a period, an exclamation point, or a question mark. This has been the industry standard for years, but many new writers aren't aware of the change because most other industries don't press the point. But you're a professional writer; if you haven't yet converted to "one space" typing, now's the time.

In the days of typewriters, an extra space was necessary to create a more defined space between sentences for the reader's eye. Typewriter fonts are monospaced—all the letters take up the same amount of space—and writers then were taught in typing class to add that extra keystroke at the end of a sentence. But computerized fonts are proportionally spaced, and a single space after a full stop is sufficient to provide a visible break.

When in doubt, turn to the *The Chicago Manual of Style*, whose official view on this issue is that there is no good reason to use two spaces after a period for work that is to be published. Obviously, this rule does not apply to personal correspondence, notes, your other job, etc.

Editors are going to upload your manuscript to a digital platform for the printer or an online publication. When they do, they'll need there to be only one space after each of your sentences. Send it to them correctly, and save them the trouble of fixing it.

Have you been using an extra space throughout your entire manuscript? Here's a quick fix to fill your two-space gaps: You can easily reformat your work with the "find/replace" function on your word-processing program. In the "find" box, type two spaces. Then in the "replace" box, type one space. As you retrain your fingers, you might want to use the find/replace function just to double-check yourself before sending new work out to editors.

How to End a Scene

When you have a scene break, center a *** or ### on your page. You can use something else if you'd like, but use a clean indicator that's easy on the eyes. Don't get too fancy, or it will be difficult for editors to format your work for the digital upload.

Naming Your Files

When you're ready to submit a short story or essay, take a minute to rename your file something appropriate for editors to see. Perhaps use your title and name (The Pond_Harris) or just the title. You can also use a key word or two from the title. The last thing you want to do is confuse editors with a placeholder title you put there during the first draft, especially if it no longer has anything to do with the work you're submitting.

WORKING IN WORD VS. PAGES

The world of publishing works in Microsoft Word, though the majority of writers I know use a Mac. You'd think that we would have integrated these two systems perfectly by now, but we haven't. Files from Pages do not easily open in a Word document system. Since every editor you will meet is working with a Word-based document system, that can cause a problem for us Mac users.

Not to worry, there are a few easy fixes available if you're in the same camp as me. Anytime you send a file as an attachment or submit your work through an electronic upload, you're going to need to send those files in a Word document, so be prepared. Whenever you complete a final draft (including proper manuscript formatting), export the file to a Word document. You'll have both the Word and the Pages files on your computer. You'll know which one is the Word file because the manuscript icon will have one corner bent down.

REMEMBER: If you need to convert your work to a Word file, do so now.

18

SUBMITTING SHORT STORIES & ESSAYS

By now you know exactly how to describe your writing project, where you'd like to send it, and how to introduce yourself. You also have a perfectly formatted manuscript on your desk ready to go. It's time to submit your work!

Nervous?

I know. I understand. It isn't easy to share your creative work with strangers. It requires you to take a leap of faith. You'll feel vulnerable and face uncertainty, but this is a necessary step to get what you want. This submission is the bridge between your creative work and publishing; this is the right path for you. Be brave enough to follow through with the process. A few things to feel great about:

1. You are sending your work to editors in a professional way. You're not just tossing something out. You've edited your prose. You're following their writers' guidelines. You're submitting this great piece of writing to someone who is actually looking for writing like yours.
2. Your writing will be read by someone who cares. Your manuscript is going to land in the hands of a devoted editor who likes writers and great writing. Editors are our partners on this journey. They'll

take you seriously, and they'll treat you kindly. They're hoping to make a match, too.

3. Nothing bad will happen if your story or essay gets rejected. You won't be blackballed from the writing industry. You won't lose your ability to create new work. You won't lose friends or love or health. In fact, you will gain something very important: credibility. Not the credibility you'll get when one of your pieces gets selected for publication but the kind of credibility you'll have among writers—street cred. That "I Put Myself Out There" badge of honor that we admire in our fellow writers. Getting a rejection means that you're in the game. You're really doing this.

WHAT'S IN A NAME

It's time to think about your byline—the name you'll use as a professional writer. Before you send anything out the door, you'll need to decide what name you'd like attached to your creative work. The obvious choice is to just use your first and last name. That might be the right decision, but maybe it's not.

Take a minute to Google your name. What comes up? If you've got a few bylines under your name already or a blog or book out there, you'll see those show up on the first page. If you don't have any writing credits yet, you might only find your Facebook page listed. Either way, you're going to see other things listed there under your name, items that don't have anything to do with "the real you."

If the items you find are other same-named people's Facebook pages and Twitter accounts or LinkedIn profiles, then go ahead and use your regular name as your professional byline name. But if the items you find attached to your name—products of those other same-named folks—are surprising in any way, you need to think about what you'd like to do next. Things I've found in a Google search of Market Coaching clients' real names: porn, racist rants, prison records, sex-offender notices, and eye-popping YouTube videos. None of the aforementioned items were from the real lives of any clients, just their "name twins." Find out what your name-twins are up to.

If anything you see connected to your name online is incongruent with who you'd like to be known as in the writing world or if your name isn't new to the writing world, then you need to make a decision. Do you want to risk people wondering if that name-twin is you, or do you want to create an identity that is unique?

If you need a name-tweak, there's a quick and easy fix. Add your middle name or middle initial, or use initials for your first and middle names. You can use your middle name instead of your first name or just make up a name. Keep Googling the combinations until you like what you find in the search results.

One more thing to think about: You'll likely want a website at some point, and that site should reflect your byline name. Check the purchase availability for your byline domain, and buy it as soon as you can, even if you don't plan to launch that website yet. I chose to use my middle name in my byline when I discovered that a well-known real-estate agent was already using windyharris.com. My website is windylynnharris.com instead.

THE FOUR DIFFERENT WAYS MANUSCRIPTS REACH THEIR DESTINATIONS

There are four distinct ways of sending your manuscript into the hands of an editor. You'll send your work by e-mail, regular mail, digital upload, or you'll be given a WordPress login password by the magazine's editor. Each magazine's preferred submission method will be listed in the writers' guidelines.

Snail-mail submissions are pretty rare these days. Uploads have become the most common practice overall, with e-mailed submissions close behind. Only a few magazines use the WordPress password system, so you might never send a submission that way. If you ever do come across this type of submission, just follow the online directions.

Since a digital upload is the most common submission situation you'll experience, let's take a closer look at that system. Magazines that use a digital upload do so because it's an easy way for them to keep track of manuscripts. Lucky for writers, it's the easiest way to submit, too.

Most editors use Submittable, but there are a few other brands out there. Digital-upload systems are embedded into a magazine's writers' guidelines, usually with a simple "submit here" button. When you click, a portal will open to a submission page. There will be boxes to fill in and a place to upload your manuscript. The boxes vary from magazine to magazine, but the most common things you'll see are:

1. Add your name/contact information here.
2. Paste your query letter here.
3. How did you hear about the magazine?

Below that will be a button that says "upload your manuscript" (or something similar). When you click, you'll be able to search your computer for a Word file. Some magazines also accept .pdf files.

One of the best things about magazines that use Submittable is the transparency it offers writers. At the time of your first Submittable upload, you will create a user account. This account allows you access to a private online page that lists every Submittable submission you have sent to editors and the status of that submission. When you submit new work via Submittable, your page will automatically reflect the action and give a status of "received." When an editor opens your document, the status changes to "in progress." When a decision is made, the status changes again to either "accepted" or "declined."

Submittable also makes it very quick and easy to withdraw a submission, should you have to. Just click the "withdraw" button next to the magazine's name. A text box will appear so you can write the editors a quick note.

THE MANUSCRIPT'S JOURNEY

Let's imagine you are sitting at a table with your polished manuscript and cover letter in front of you on the computer screen. You know where you're going to send these pages, and you've double-checked the submission guidelines. The magazine you've selected asks that all submissions be e-mailed, so you open your e-mail program and begin. You fill in the contact information and paste your pages into the body. You press that "send" button and hear that unmistakable *whooosh*! Your work is on its way. Let's look at what happens to your submission once it's out of your hands.

Your submission will arrive at its destination immediately (unless you're sending by post), but it might be weeks or months before it gets read. Many magazines have a backlog of submissions. Be patient; know that the process has started. Go write something new. Read magazines you might query someday. Visit your local library, and see what short-story or essay collections they have on the shelves.

Eventually, someone is going to open your document(s). It might be the person you intended, but it might just as likely be someone else at the magazine. It might be an MFA student or a volunteer editor hunting through the submissions for promising work. Whoever does the job, here's her task: This first peek is an initial credibility screening. This person is looking to see if you sent the kind of writing that she actually publishes (so much of what gets sent isn't!), she's looking to see if you've sent the right length of prose (so much isn't!), and she's looking for the overall professionalism of the submission package.

Lucky for you, you're going to nail all of these things and pass this first screening with ease. Your work will move on to the second phase of the process: the read. The first person to open your documents might be the only one who reads your work, or your prose might get passed through many hands before a decision is made. Some literary magazines have a large editorial board that meets once a month. Editors bring their favorite submission to the meeting, and everyone works together to choose the most cohesive collection of great submissions from what is available.

Your work can get rejected at different stages throughout the process. During the first read, your writing might get rejected immediately for reasons beyond your control:

- The magazine recently published something with a similar topic or theme.
- They've already accepted something for an *upcoming* issue with a similar topic or theme.
- They are near the end of the selection for the next issue, and the piece you submitted is too long for the space they have left.
- They are near the end of the selection for the next issue, and they have already selected enough short stories (or essays).

If you receive a quick rejection letter, think about these auto-rejection situations. You've likely fallen into one of these areas.

If your submission passes that first glance, your writing has a shot at getting published. Your work will be given a thoughtful read. If the first reader likes what you've sent, he will send it along to the other people making decisions at the magazine. If he is the only decision-maker on board, that editor will set your work in a pile with other great items and make a decision based on the overall content available to him. Someone might even let you know that you've made it to the next round of decisions. This "thorough-read period" is also where you might get rejected. Perhaps the editor doesn't think the work you submitted is a fit for the magazine, or maybe he feels your prose isn't ready for publication yet. In either case, you'll be notified with a generic rejection letter, and then you can move on to other opportunities.

But back to the positive scenario: Your work is in that nice pile of submissions that the editor really likes. Your prose is near the finish line. The only thing standing between you and an acceptance letter is the fact that there are many other writers out there producing great work, too. The top literary magazines can only publish about 3 percent of the work that comes in. If you receive a rejection at this stage, it is likely for similar reasons to those quick rejections. Your work was good enough, but it didn't fit the very specific needs of this magazine for the upcoming issue. It didn't shine the brightest out of all the gems available.

Now let's talk about all of those times in your future where your work *does* make the cut; the moments when an editor selects your prose for publication. The editorial team will take into consideration things like overall physical layout of the magazine and flow of the included pieces as part of the decision process. The editor will send you an acceptance notice by e-mail as soon as she has a final plan. This is a critical time for the magazine, since they've also sent rejection letters. They're counting on you to accept their terms so that they can move on to the production phase. It's customary for you to respond with an acceptance of terms within twenty-four hours.

Your short story or essay is now in production. First, there will be formatting for a digital upload to either the online platform or the printer. Copyediting comes next. Then an editor will have a galley copy printed; if necessary, just to check the overall formatting and editing. Some print magazines will send you a galley to sign off on; others won't include you in this part of the process at all.

Then comes publication day.

If the magazine is going to publish your work online, you'll see it happen on publication day. They'll usually tell you that date at the same time they accept your work. You might or might not be reminded on publication day, so mark your calendar.

If your work is appearing in a print magazine, you'll need to watch your mailbox for those contributor copies. They could take up to a week or more to arrive after the publication date. The magazine will start promoting the new issue online before you even see your copy. But then your copy will show up at your house, and you'll see your writing in print with your name right there below the title.

Whichever medium your work appears in, spread the news about your byline through social media and mention the magazine by name. Add the credit to your website—if you have one—and add the new information to your third-person bio.

Celebrate your success!

How Many Magazines Should You Query at a Time?

Send your work to five different editors (or more if you've got time to research additional markets) the first time you send a piece out the door.

If you're hungry for a first byline, send your story out to twenty editors that are accepting simultaneous submissions.

This number will change as your goals do, of course. There will be times when you're targeting a specific magazine. Maybe you're sure a certain story of yours is perfect for *Guernica*. When you've got your eye on a prize like that, only send your work to that one magazine and wait patiently for a response. If they pass, you can always send that piece to five other editors.

How Long is This Going to Take?

Some editors will get back to you with a decision in the first couple of weeks, and others will take several months. You might get some hints about the response time in the writers' guidelines, but you might not. Wait at least three months before raising an eyebrow. Yes, that long. Don't worry; you're a busy person. You've got new things to write. Just keep working, and let this process play out.

I once had a piece accepted after nine months. The essay was only still for sale because I'd given up on it and had stopped sending it out. I liked the essay, but it had already been widely rejected. I had tucked it in with other stories that I might or might not revisit. When I got the acceptance letter, I read my work again and realized that I was proud to have it published. I liked it a lot. The editor told me she'd been hanging on to it, waiting for the right time of year to publish it.

In another instance, I had an essay accepted after fourteen months of silence. Similar comments from the editor! The lesson: Just because you don't hear something right away doesn't mean your story has been forgotten. It might mean he likes it but is trying to find the right time for it.

Once you get an acceptance letter, it could be anywhere from one week to one year before your work gets published. Online magazines have faster production times, but sometimes they acquire writing months ahead of when they need it. Print publications have a much longer lead time, and you could easily wait a full year from first submission to published copy in a magazine and sometimes longer.

"When people tell me they write for themselves but they don't submit, I usually nod and smile—at least at first. But it doesn't take me long to encourage even the shyest writer to work towards submitting. I wonder if these writers are truly writing for themselves or if it is fear of rejection that keeps them from submitting.

"I don't deny that it's hard, especially at first, to face the rejection that is ultimately part of the writer's life. It takes tremendous strength to stand up and say: My voice has value. My story means something.

"There is no magic formula to overcoming fear. However, you can build resistance to it, and in this way, slowly but surely, work to overcome it. The trick is that you can't let the first wave (or the second or third or the hundredth!) knock you down. But don't focus on all the waves that will come. Just keep standing through this wave. Over time, you'll find that the longer you stand strong, the more firmly rooted you will become.

"And you need to keep standing, keep writing, [and] keep submitting. Your voice matters. Art heals us in the writing and heals others in the reading. Your voice belongs in the world. Keep standing, and let the wave wash past you. When it does, you might look around and see the others out there with you. We're all in this together."

—JENNIFER KIRCHER CARR

HOW TO PRESENT & MAIL YOUR MANUSCRIPT

For each submission method, there is an industry standard for presenting your work. Here's what you need to know.

Snail Mail Submissions

1. Paperclip the pages of your manuscript together. Never use staples (editors need to make quick copies of your manuscript for editorial boards).
2. Fold your SASE (self-addressed stamped envelope) into thirds, and tuck it behind your manuscript, under the paperclip. The SASE is addressed to *you*. Write the magazine's address in the top-left corner, and attach a stamp.
3. Place your signed cover letter on top of the manuscript. Remember to sign your name at the bottom.
4. Fewer than five pages can be folded into a standard business envelope. Five pages or more should be mailed flat in a manila envelope.
5. Mail your manuscripts first class (with a regular stamp). Never certify or register a submission.

E-Mail Submissions

1. Begin the e-mail message with your cover letter, minus your contact information.
2. Include your manuscript's text in the e-mail's body, below the cover letter (unless the writers' guidelines specifically asked for manuscripts to be sent as attachments, which is rare).
3. In the subject line, write the words "Query: Title of Your Story." If the magazine's writers' guidelines give you other instructions, follow those instead. Some ask that you specify fiction or nonfiction in the subject line.

Digital Upload Submissions

All uploads have an online form that gives you a place to enter your contact information and cover letter. You do not need to change your cover letter to a Word file or PDF; just copy and paste it into the correct box. Your manuscript does need to be a Word file or a PDF. When you select the option to upload your work, you will be able to select the correct file type.

COPYRIGHT LAW

Copyright is the legal protection of your written work. It's granted instantly each time you write a new short story or essay. You don't need to mail anything to the United States Copyright Office to protect your writing. As soon as you put your name and the date on your written work, you are protected by the copyright law.

When you enter into a short-story or essay contract, you are granting the magazine permission to use your intellectual property for a limited time. The copyright law assumes that writers are selling onetime rights when they enter a contract, unless the writer and publisher agree otherwise. Typically, the duration of copyright is the author's life plus fifty to one-hundred years (in other words, copyright expires fifty to one-hundred years after the author's death).

Don't put a copyright symbol (circle with a "c" inside of it) on your written work. Editors and publishers consider placing the copyright symbol anywhere on your manuscript to be a sure sign of an amateur. It signals that you don't understand how copyright works and probably don't understand how contracts work either. Some editors are even offended by the symbol on your prose since it implies that you don't trust the person you've sent it to.

The Rights You Sell

When a publication offers to buy your piece of writing, you're not actually selling the piece of writing. You're selling specific rights governing the use of your piece. There are many rights available for you to sell, including print, electronic, film, foreign, and translation. In the absence of a contract or any stated rights, it's usually understood that you're selling "first" rights, but it never hurts to make sure. This is your property, after all, and you are in charge of managing the rights to your work.

Here are the rights you'll come across when selling short stories and essays.

First Serial Rights (or First Rights)

When you sell first rights, you're selling a publication the right to be the first place to publish the material. This right holds the most monetary value in short stories and essays. A first-rights contract often comes with a specified period of time that the publication would like to have your work exclusively, usually 90–120 days. After the contract period, unless you've granted other rights or licenses, all copyrighted material reverts back to you. You can then sell other rights to that work, which is called "selling a reprint."

Sometimes first fights are referred to as FNASR, which stands for "first North American serial rights." This term is added to denote a geographical location. This is an important thing to notice since signing an FNASR contract means that you still retain first rights in other geographic locations. With so many wonderful international magazines available to approach, this could be important to you. Consider first British rights, first European rights, and first Australian rights (to name just a few).

Publications consider material posted online to be previously published and therefore unqualified to meet a first-rights contract. This includes work you post on Facebook, your website, or your blog, even if you have a small audience there. Don't post any short story or essay online that you'd like to send to editors. If you already have, you can still sell the piece to a journal, but you will only be able to sell it as a reprint.

Reprints (Second Serial Rights)

What do you do once the rights to a piece revert back to you? You sell it again! You can never sell the first rights of a piece more than once, but you can sell the reprint rights as soon as your first contract has expired. There is no limit to the amount of times you can resell a piece like this, so a single essay or short story can appear in many journals. I've sold essays up to four times. Each publication had a completely different audience, so everyone was happy. Try to get at least two bylines out of every great piece you write.

When you offer serial rights, you are telling the publication that first rights for the piece have been sold but that the publication can purchase the right from you to print the piece again as a reprint. Or, to phrase it differently, the publication can purchase the right to print the piece a second time. Reprint contracts are always spelled out carefully, so do take the time to read them thoroughly. Make sure that you will, once again, get your rights back at the end of the contract period. Reprint rights pay less than first rights, typically half of what a journal would pay for first rights.

Electronic Rights

Online journals purchase first electronic rights, which means that they are buying the right to be the first to provide the material electronically. Many journals that have both online and print publications acquire the first electronic and print rights at the same time. This happens often enough that you should assume that's the case, even if your journal didn't specify both rights anywhere in the guidelines or contract. However, you should always clarify with the journal what you're selling.

If the publication that purchased your first rights was a print-only effort, you can sell first electronic rights separately. If you are offering first electronic rights to a piece that has been exclusively in print already, it's customary to mention this in your query letter. The publication might consider it a reprint at that point, or they might offer to purchase first electronic rights.

All Rights

Selling all rights to your work means that you are giving up any future rights to the piece. Nothing will revert back to you at the end of the contract period because there is no end to the contract period. This is common when selling greeting-card writing (and in some other industries), but I'd caution you against selling all rights for a short story or an essay. Should you wish to include that same piece in an anthology or collection of your works later on, you would have to purchase back the rights from the publication that purchased all rights from you.

Anthology Rights

This gives the publisher of an anthology—a collection of short writing—the right to publish your piece in their collection. Anthologies often purchase reprint material. Many magazines that put out annual "best of" collections negotiate anthology rights with authors whose work has appeared in their magazines.

THE COMMON CONTRACT

Contracts for short stories and personal essays are interesting in that they often don't exist. What I mean is that they usually don't exist in the traditional sense that other contracts do. For book projects—fiction or nonfiction—you'll have a print or digital contract sent your way with a line for your signature. Sometimes this happens for the sale of a short story or essay, too. But more often than not, the contracts for short stories and essays are brief.

When selling short work, it's very common to receive an e-mail from an editor that goes something like this (in lieu of a formal contract): "Thank you for your submission of 'Who Wants to Kill a Millionaire.' We would like to publish it in the June 15 edition of *Alfred Hitchcock Mystery Magazine.*" That's it, end of contract. There might be another line reiterating what you'll receive in payment if you have money or contributor copies coming your way, but other than that—done.

The reason for this is that the meat of a short story and essay contract has already been stated in the writers' guidelines. This is where you read that the publication wants an exclusive for 120 days. That's where they stated that they will archive your work electronically. It's where the publications said they'd e-mail you a PDF of the magazine. You've read the guidelines, so you already know what you'll receive in exchange for publication. It is assumed that you "pre-agree" to the terms by submitting your work.

Know what rights you are selling before you answer that e-mail and accept. You own all rights to your work (ex: print, electronic, foreign, film) until you agree to a contract. Double-check those online writers' guidelines. Make sure you know when your rights will revert back to you, if ever. If you have questions, ask the editor in a polite e-mail response:

> Thank you for offering to include my story in the June 15 publication. I'd like to make sure I understand your terms before I agree. How long would you like to have an exclusive on this work?

My advice: Get paid *something* but not necessarily money. All forms of payment have value to your writing career. Exposure and experience are both important pieces to the overall writing puzzle. Revisit your goals regularly. Decide what is important to you, and submit your work accordingly.

GETTING ORGANIZED

When selling short prose, you'll typically send your work to more than one editor at a time. That can be hard to keep track of if you aren't diligent, so be as organized as you can in this process. It's important to keep track of the dates you submit, where you submitted, and the response. Beyond that, you might also keep track of the submission formats and the editors' names.

I like to keep it simple. Consider using the following submission tracker, or come up with one of your own (I know many writers who use Duotrope's online submission tracker, one feature that comes with the $5 monthly subscription). I print out a new submission tracker for every piece of writing I'd like to sell. I fill in the title and word count and then list any appropriate categories. I send new work to at least five editors at a time. Sometimes more. As the responses roll in, I note them on the page with the date. A rejection would get an *R 12/5/17*, for instance. When someone offers to publish my work, I draw a smiley face in that last column. Then I drop down to the bottom two lines and fill in the specifics of the contract.

SUBMISSION TRACKER

TITLE OF PIECE

_____

WORD COUNT _____ CATEGORIES _____

DATE	PUBLICATION	RESPONSE

PUBLISHED: _____

_____

_____

Every Monday I sit at my desk and check over the latest rejections from journal editors. I make decisions about where I should send my stories next and then follow my five-step process to get that work back out the door. Increase your chances of publication by keeping each piece of work circulating to at least five editors until you receive an acceptance letter.

Allow a minimum of three months to hear about a submission. After that time, it's okay to write a polite letter or e-mail inquiring about the status of the manuscript.

Nudging Editors

When three months have passed without any word from an editor, check the writers' guidelines. If they don't mention anything about taking several months to respond, then you should send the editor an e-mail. When you do, assume the best. Perhaps the editor is still reading your work. Maybe it's even at the last round of decisions. He might be typing up your acceptance letter right now.

Be polite. Editors know each other; they talk to each other. Don't ever risk giving yourself a bad reputation by blasting off a *Why haven't you read my work, you lazy editor?* Instead, send a simple note, something like this:

> Hi Ms. Johnson,
>
> I'm just checking in on my January 7 submission of "This Great Story." Are you still making decisions about the piece?

Editors always respond to this type of note. Usually, you'll get something back like:

> Dear Ms. Harris,
>
> We appreciate your inquiry. We have a long list of stories we're still considering. We will get back to you with an answer as soon as possible. Thank you for your patience.

I suspect they will check their slush pile and read your work soon after. Even if they don't, you've had a chance to behave like a professional writer again. That kind of thing is remembered in this business.

WHAT TO DO WHEN YOU GET AN ACCEPTANCE LETTER

Celebrate (obviously)! And then, after carefully reading everything, accept their offer. You should send an e-mail back to the editor within twenty-four hours, telling him that you accept. He's waiting to see if you're really on board so he can move to the production phase. My note usually looks like this:

> Hi Ms. Johnson,
>
> Thank you for the opportunity to be a part of *Pithead Chapel*'s May 17 edition. I'm looking forward to publication day.

That's it. Quick and professional.

Next, you need to inform any editor still holding your work that you've sold the piece. Again, this needs to happen within twenty-four hours so that editor can stop the process of reading or discussing your piece. Your work could be at the last round of decision, for all you know. The editor might be trying to decide between your story and another. The sooner you can pull your work, the easier his job will be. That letter looks like this:

> Dear Mr. Thompson,
>
> I wanted to inform you right away that my short story, "A Town Built on Salt," was accepted by another journal. I plan to send you another story in the future. I'd like to work together one day.

This letter accomplished two things: 1) It shows the editor you are a trustworthy professional who cares about the submission process, and 2) it shows the editor that your story was a good one and that he missed out. Maybe next time he'll remember your name and read your work a little faster.

Invoices and Payments

Once you have a publishing contract solidified, you need to keep track of when, where, and how much this magazine is going to pay you. Normally you'll receive a check and your contributor copies right on time, but once in a while you have to remind an editor that you haven't been paid. It happens. Wait until thirty days have elapsed from the original projected pay date, and then send a polite e-mail about the matter. Your note might go something like this:

> Hi Mr. Jacobs,
>
> I'm inquiring about payment for the June 25 publication of my short story, "Mrs. Anderson's Jesus." Do you know if the check has already been sent?

Consider using the following invoice tracker, or create something else that works well for you. If you like keeping all of your records online, you might prefer creating a spreadsheet.

INVOICE & PAYMENT TRACKER

TITLE OF PIECE	PUBLICATION	PUB DATE	CONTRACT TERMS AMOUNT	PAID?

Writing & Selling Short Stories & Personal Essays

YOUR TURN: SUBMIT YOUR WORK LIKE A PRO

The goal is to submit your work professionally and have an editor offer a publishing contract. To have the best chance at success, give each story or essay your full attention during your submission time. Here's a checklist to follow when you sit down to send your work:

- Double-check that you're happy with the final draft of your story or essay.
- Distance yourself from the work for a minute, and search out all of the possible categories and topics.
- Find five viable markets to query. Refer to your category list for comparisons.
- Write a great cover letter to a specific editor for a specific reason.
- Format your manuscript.
- Read the writers' guidelines for submissions, and follow them exactly. Watch for the words "simultaneous submissions" and "multiple submissions." Adjust your query plan accordingly.
- Record your submission in some organized way.

When you're ready, press that "send" button (or put that letter in the mail)!

KEEP TRACK OF YOUR WORK

Interested in downloading trackers like the ones featured in this book? Visit www.writersdigest.com/writing-selling-short-stories-personal-essays.

19

HOW TO DEAL WITH REJECTION

The very first rejection letter I ever received is pinned to the corkboard near my desk. It came from *Good Housekeeping* in January of 2006. I'd sent them a personal essay titled "Muddle Age." It's a small piece of paper, about one-third of a sheet. The company's logo is printed at the top in green.

This rejection letter is a badge of honor for me, proving that I was brave enough to send my work out to the world that very first time. I keep it nearby as encouragement: *Keep at this—keep sharing my voice. Keep putting my words into the hands of strangers.*

It hasn't gotten any easier to submit my writing. I feel vulnerability creep up every single time. I comfort myself with the facts: 1) I firmly believe the piece I'm sending out is ready for publication and has been edited to my fullest ability, and 2) I am sending my work to someone looking for submissions like mine.

I also know that everything will be just fine if I get a rejection letter. I've received hundreds of rejections from magazines over the years, and I'm still here, writing stories and essays and pushing them out the door. Rejection isn't going to stop you from submitting your work, either.

There's an interesting fact about rejection letters that I want to share with you: Rejections are among the most boring pieces of communication on Earth. Most magazines have a bland rejection template. Sometimes they fill in your name, and sometimes they don't. For example, that rejection letter I received from *Good Housekeeping* reads:

> Dear Contributor:
>
> Thank you for your submission. We read it with interest. Unfortunately, it does not meet our editorial needs at this time. We appreciate you thinking of *Good Housekeeping* and wish you the best [of luck in] placing your material elsewhere.
>
> Sincerely,
> The Editors

Three months later I received this letter from *Complete Woman*:

> Dear Windy:
>
> Thank you for submitting the enclosed materials for our consideration. While we certainly enjoyed your work, it does not meet with our current editorial needs. Please feel free to submit more of your work in the future. We appreciate your interest in our publication.
>
> Sincerely,
> Bonnie L. Krueger,
> Editor-in-Chief

You'd read similar variations of "no thank you" if you flipped through the seventeen other rejections I received that year, and you'd read more of the same if you saw the letters I got last week. You will never be judged or harassed or made to feel small in a rejection letter. This business doesn't work like that. You'll feel a sting because you were turned down, but you won't be stung by the words of an editor. In fact, you might even read a rejection letter and smile because there is something in this business called a *good* rejection letter.

GOOD REJECTIONS

Good rejection letters are the ones where an editor has stopped the busy machine of magazine production for a moment and written you a personal note of encouragement. It might be a few lines added to the bottom of a form letter or perhaps an expansion of a magazine's basic e-mail rejection. Either way, this note is important. It is meant to make you stop your busy machine, too.

A note of personal encouragement is a big green flashing light that indicates your writing stood out among the hundreds of other submissions this editor recently received. Your work was so promising that someone took the time to say hello and give you a thumbs-up. You didn't make the final cut, but the editor wanted you to know that there's something pretty awesome about your work.

Take a minute to let that compliment sink in. Let it warm your writer bones and fill your writer lungs. You deserve that wide smile across your face.

The custom of writing personal bits of encouragement to writers is generations old. The masters we've studied received both generic and encouraging rejections along the way. I like to keep track of any personal rejection I receive in a file marked "Submit Again." This editor likes my style. When I send them a new story, I'll mention our prior contact in the cover letter. I also put a star beside that rejection when I log it into my submission tracker. If I've received a good rejection or two for a piece making the rounds of submission, I know not to stop and revise, even if I rack up a long list of rejections. The piece will find a home; it's only a matter of time.

Should I Thank the Editor for the Rejection?

You can if you'd like, but it isn't necessary and not expected as part of being a polite writer. I've replied "thank you" to some editors who have sent me personal notes but not all of them.

Can I Resubmit the Same Story Again if I Revise It?

Don't send an editor a revised edition of a story they've rejected. Move on to other markets. If an editor is interested enough in your piece to look at it a second time, they'll ask for revisions instead of sending a rejection letter.

Should I Send Them a Different Story?

Absolutely! As soon as you have something appropriate for their magazine, send it. Don't let too much time go by. Make sure you mention your prior contact in your new cover letter.

True Rejection Stories from Fellow Writers

"My dad is a writer, and while I was in grade school and junior high, he had been writing and submitting short stories to various magazines across the country. He would give me a few to read, gauge my reaction, telling me to be honest if something didn't make sense or sounded off. He treated me like the budding writer I had become, and I was happy for the experience. Dad would then mail the stories off and continue writing while he waited patiently for a response.

"'Always expect a rejection letter,' he would say, tacking to the corkboard in his office the latest 'thanks, but no thanks' response from some magazine. 'There are millions of us writers out there, so keep that in mind when sending something off. Then you'll be pleasantly surprised when you do get accepted.'

"I didn't start submitting my writing until earlier this year, and when I did, I sent out the pieces to one place only and they accepted them the next day for their upcoming issue. I was floored, expecting an e-mail of rejection instead. Actually, I was hoping for a rejection to see how I'd handle it. Then I considered myself lucky, thinking that the next time I submit, lightning wouldn't strike twice. I was right, not just once but twice in the same week. These rejections stung slightly for a few seconds; then what I'd been taught for twenty-five years kicked in—it's the nature of the beast. I went back to the stories I sent out and started reworking them where I felt they needed it most. It was cathartic and exciting because I … already had a good idea of where the words didn't sound quite right or where more skin on the bones was needed. Fix it up; send it back out; keep writing.

"If I were to get sullen about every rejection letter to come my way, well, there would probably be a long, cluttered trail of empty Ben & Jerry's containers, Snickers wrappers, and donut boxes leading to me, facedown on a sidewalk somewhere. Instead, I just remember what my dad always said, still says: 'These things happen, kid. Just gotta start over and keep at it.'"

—Hillary Umland

"Most of my submission stories end with the sting of rejection, but some also incorporate 'acceptance remorse.' Remember that Groucho Marx line, the one where he says he wouldn't want to belong to any club that would have him as a member? Many times in the past, I would submit a piece simultaneously to several journals. Among the group I'd include one dream journal, the equivalent of a high-school senior's 'reach school.' All literary journals are selective, and my dream journals are even more so. I knew my chance of being accepted by my dream journal was exceedingly slim, but I figured, why not try? Inevitably, one of the other journals would respond first, accepting the piece, and I always regretted not giving my dream journal an exclusive first shot. Sure, I had as much chance of being accepted by one of my dream journals as winning the lottery, but if I continued as I had, I'd never know for sure.

"My latest episode of 'Adventures in Submitting' began in January and resolved eight months later, in autumn. I wrote a humorous/heartfelt (or at least I thought so) essay in the form of a list and wanted to submit it to a certain dream journal. The information on their submission page was written in a breezy tone and this made me think my piece might have a fair chance there.

"I pressed 'submit.' I waited. Winter transitioned into spring. I waited. Spring eased into summer and no word. By mid-summer the piece had been tied up for so long, I figured I should [implement] a Plan B. I decided to submit the essay to another journal, a lovely journal, a journal I'd be proud to appear in but one not as well-known as my dream journal. I hadn't totally given up on my original plan, but I gave myself permission to submit to this second journal because I told myself there was no way the lovely journal would get back to me before my dream journal.

"The information on Duotrope, an online service that tracks statistics on literary magazines' turnaround times, led me to believe that I would hear from my dream literary journal any day. The dream journal had just rejected a submission sent in fifty days after mine. This made me hopeful. After all, why would they hold off on deciding on my piece, which they'd had longer, if it wasn't still in the running? Still, I couldn't help but wonder if they were leading me on. I complained to my husband, 'It's been 259 days! If they are going to reject me, why don't they just do it and end my suspense already?!' To which my husband replied, 'Honey, if anyone deserves to be rejected, it's you.'

"The next day author Laila Lalami gave a reading at the university where I am working toward my MFA, and as I waited to get my photo snapped with her, I glanced at my phone. There it was: an acceptance. From the lovely journal. I've been told that in the submissions game it's first come, first served, but I couldn't let go of the possibility of being published by my dream journal. The lovely journal's editor asked if my piece was still available. Was it? I sent an e-mail directly to the editor of the dream journal, bypassing the traditional submission system. I explained to the dream journal's editor how much I would *love* to have them pick up my piece but that I would need to know that same day in order to be fair to the lovely journal.

"A few hours later, the dream journal's editor sent me a rejection. By that time, I was so glad to know one way or the other that the rejection didn't sting. (That's a lie; it killed me.) But I had a wonderful home for the piece in the lovely journal. And in their rejection note, the dream journal had asked me to submit other work. I sent them another piece that same evening. I'm still waiting."

—Susan Lerner

Note: The story Susan is talking about went on to be nominated for a Pushcart Prize that year!

"When I finally got around to writing a short story, my goal was simple: Write a story that readers would enjoy and, if published, wouldn't stalk me throughout my life with humiliation and shame. I didn't know much about literary magazines then. Over the years I'd read some of the more acclaimed ones, but most of my exposure had been limited to collections. I sent my nearly 6,000-word story to a top-tier lit mag and of course was left wondering a few months later where to send it next. I wish I could say I had a letter from that very first rejection. My status merely changed on their website. This is when I decided to incorporate prospect research into publication and to treat rejection as part of the business of publishing. I started looking for places that fit my writing and my publishing goals.

"I managed to find prospective publication venues, new writing, and to make new connections in the small and independent-press literary world in several ways. I first followed the University of Iowa MFA's Twitter feed, as well as the literary magazines and presses it followed. This led me down a rabbit warren of possibilities and extraordinary reading material, and it introduced me to writers and editors. I selected Iowa because at the time, Iowa was the one I knew. A new writer can select most any literary magazine, press, editor, MFA program, author, or agent and follow the thread to new connections. Next, I looked up where authors I liked and identified with had published early in their careers, and I read those publications. … This lead to learning about other authors and meeting them on social media and learning about more publications and joining social-media groups about writing and publication. For data about submissions and calendars for opportunities, I subscribed to databases, listservs, and blogs about publications and contests such as Aerogramme Writers' Studio, Duotrope, *The Review Review*, Paul McVeigh's blog, *Poets & Writers*, The (Submission) Grinder, and *Writer's Digest*.

"While I was learning about this vast new world, I targeted two places, including one in particular I had run across years ago when they were relatively new. It had a classic, retro design and typography, and they published breathtaking stories with a quick response time that included feedback for submissions [of] up to 3,000 words. I cut my story to the bone and submitted 2,079 words to *Bartleby Snopes*.

"*Bartleby Snopes* declined my submission with good ink—what my friends and I call a good rejection letter. Rick Taliaferro, the associate editor at the time, complimented my aptitude and pointed out why the story's resolution was unsatisfactory in relationship to the initial conflict. This simple, fatal dissonance was not evident to me until Rick mentioned it, and I realized there were two storylines fracturing the narrative. I cut the original story essentially in half, revised it, and sent each one to two other places that published them immediately. I am as grateful to *Bartleby Snopes* for their rejection as I am to *Thrice Fiction* and *Dew on the Kudzu* for welcoming them. I ended up with seventy-seven drafts of those stories, and when *Bartleby Snopes* called for open submissions for new editors, I applied. They accepted."

—April Bradley

"If you are a writer, you will be rejected. This is not just a painful and inevitable fact of the profession; it is also painfully essential. Rejections force writers into uncomfortable and vulnerable spaces. It means persevering and considering that the work you thought was perfect is not quite finished yet. Eventually, you'll realize that no work is ever perfect and that isn't what matters anyways. What matters is if it lands. Does it resonate with the reader? Don't get me wrong—it should be good. It should be the literal best you can make it; but that will always only be half the equation. The trick to getting your work published is matching it with the right journal, the right editor, and ultimately, the right readers. Take, for instance, when I submitted what could loosely be considered a 'ghost story' to a small but respectable literary journal and got the following response: 'We're not keen on ghost stories and prefer that when a main character dies that the story dies with her or him.' Fair enough, right? That rejection might have deterred me if I'd allowed it. But that same month, *The Missouri Review* released their 'Ghosts' issue (Summer 2013), proving that at least one editor out there was keen on ghost stories. I tried again, considered every rejection with a critical eye, [and] made changes as necessary, and eventually my story was published."

—Brianne M. Kohl

"'The truth is [that] rejection letters are always a blow, like someone threw cold water on your face or you fell while performing on stage in front of your parents and two-hundred almost-strangers or your best friend forgot your birthday. The truth is that rejection hurts! But when you are in love with your craft, it doesn't stop you. As writers we are compelled to write, so we pick ourselves up, dust ourselves off, carve out the time, and persevere until that letter arrives that says, 'We love your writing and want to publish your piece in our next edition!' And then we start all over again!"

—Dr. Trish Dolasinski

"In my experience, one of the most important lessons about rejection is that one may receive many, many 'form rejections' without ever having any real correspondence with a reader or an editor. This is why the journals that offer feedback or editors who offer explanations for the rejection are so instructive for the emerging writer. I was a lucky beginner because I had instructive feedback on some of my rejections when I first started to submit to journals. One journal in particular sent, along with the kind rejection, excerpts from the notes of each of the four readers who had considered my work from the slush pile. I could see in their comments that they didn't necessarily reject my piece for the same reasons, and, more importantly, I had proof that they were 'real people'—invested, knowledgeable, discerning, and supportive of my efforts. And I had proof that four people had read my work! Having these comments in my literary pocket gave me such confidence. To know that editors were actually digesting my work, weighing my words, and considering my craft decisions was the best kind of rejection, and this information gave me another portal through which I could resee and then revise my work."

—Jolene McIlwain

"Ask any short-fiction writer who actively submits stories which kind of rejections bug them the most, and you'll get a range of responses. My pet peeves run a gamut. I'm fine with a curt form rejection as long as it comes quickly. A few weeks and no hard feelings. But more than a few months without even an apology for the wait? Sorry but that's rude. I also find generic praise-filled rejections that end with tepid 'we'd love to read more in the future' sign-offs highly suspect. If they really liked my stuff, I'd prefer something specific in the rejection to indicate they actually read the story. Otherwise, no more barking up that tree again, especially if they charge reading fees. My best defense [against] rejection-frustration is to send out one submission for every rejection as it comes in, immediately, if possible. It's a good way to keep hope alive, if only to tread water in the same place."

—Alice Kaltman

"I got another rejection today. It was a standard form rejection— nothing special. I logged it into my tracking system, an action that gives me an odd satisfaction. The practical nature of it somehow helps take the sting out of the rejection. I feel like the rejections are like sonar on the bottom of the ocean floor—I send out my signal; I receive back a signal: *You are here. You are writing.* These rejections are my touchstone with the literary world. This was a round hole for my square peg, and I need to keep sending my signals out until I find the right fit. I will only find that right fit if I keep on sending."

—Jennifer Kircher Carr

"After a story has garnered a few rejections, there is a tendency to believe that it must not be good, that the writer ought to substantially revise the story or worse, abandon it altogether. This is unfortunate. It may be the case if you're new to writing, but if you've been at it awhile, published a fair body of work, and believe in your story, you may want to disabuse yourself of this notion.

"I had a story I'd worked on for several months. A rather unusual story, I really loved it and believed in it nonetheless. When it came time to send it out, I aimed pretty high. This was in the days before Submittable, and I spent a lot of time and energy printing out my story, writing cover letters, licking stamps. Months later, the rejections began flowing in, form rejections, some witheringly [opening] with, 'Dear Writer.' I don't recall getting any personal rejections, much less any constructive feedback.

"Each time the story was rejected, I went back in and looked for something to change to improve its chances. I'd lost my belief in the story, began to doubt every sentence, every word choice, every comma. I made big, sweeping changes to the POV. I changed tenses from past to present [and then changed them] back to past. I truly came to hate the story, and after thirty-seven rejections (you read that right), I finally gave up and stopped sending it out.

"A couple of years passed. I had another piece I liked that was a bit more experimental in form. I sent it to the editor of a long-coveted journal. After several months, I received one of my kindest rejections to date. The editor said he really loved the story but had chosen a somewhat similar story already for the issue and [asked whether I] could … send something else. I was instructed to put 'solicited story' on my cover letter. I was so excited but didn't have anything else to send! Knowing that journal staffs can change, I really wanted to strike while the iron was hot, while this editor was still in charge.

"I dredged up the only other story I had available at the time, the oft-rejected story (well, the several versions of it I had in my documents folder). I discovered I still loved most of the original version, the one I'd worked so hard on and believed in before all the rejections.

"You guessed it. The editors loved it and enthusiastically accepted it. It remains one of the publications I'm most proud of. This story went on to be anthologized in a terrific collection showcasing 'provocative' women writers. I came away from that experience finally understanding that rejections and acceptances are often about finding the right fit. If you believe in your story, there's an editor out there who will believe in it, too. Don't give up on it."

—Kathy Fish

"Over the years of writing and submitting work, I've learned that rejection doesn't necessarily mean no, but rather 'not yet, not this market.' Market research and persistence is the key to becoming successfully published. A few examples from my own experience:

"In 2012, I wrote a flash piece called 'Haboob Season' for the *Paris Review* contest, 'Dog Days of Summer.' I didn't place in that contest, so I continued to submit the story to five more markets, all of which rejected me, including one who told me they really disliked the ending. Without making any major changes (I loved the ending!), I entered the piece in *WOW! Women on Writing*'s Flash Fiction contest. A couple of months later, I was notified that I had reached the semi-finalist stage. Then I received an e-mail saying I was a finalist, and on one lovely morning a few days later, I learned I had won first place! *WOW! Women on Writing* published that story, along with awarding me a nice cash prize.

"In 2014, I wrote an essay called 'Mapping the Body' that I sent to *Hunger Mountain* as my submission for their themed issue on the body. Perfect match, right? Not quite. The editors sent me a nice rejection saying they debated a long time before deciding not to use the piece, so I submitted the essay to four more markets and received nothing but form rejections. Then I sent it to *Hippocampus Magazine*. Not only did *Hippocampus* accept my essay for publication; they nominated it for [the] 2015 Pushcart Prize!"

—Jeanne Lyet Gassman

"There is such a thing as 'good ink,' and a rejection can be something to celebrate. Editors are busy people—if they take time to write a note, you can trust they mean what they say. Even a form rejection is a good thing because it means you are putting yourself out there, taking a chance."

—Elizabeth Pettie

"Rejections can be what used to be called a 'PRS'—a printed rejection slip—and those are like a blank face or a cold shoulder. Luckily, they mean as little as an anonymous comment on the Internet. They don't reflect a thing about your work or about the real you. Ignore them, and keep on going.

"Then there are the rejections that teach you something you did not know before about your own work. Sometimes you believe you've paid attention to theme or language or character, while a reader didn't feel it come through. Then you can go back through your work with these fresh eyes implanted in your skull and have one of those wonderful 'Aha!' moments."

—Savannah Thorne

"Rejections are an inevitable byproduct of acceptances. Show me a published writer, and I'll show you someone who knows what rejection feels like. It just comes with the territory. And rejection doesn't have to be the automatic negative we think it is. After all, it doesn't mean the end of the road for your piece or for your opportunity to work with a particular publication.

"For example, a piece of mine was returned to me in what is typically called a 'revise and resubmit' request. The editors were rejecting the piece as it was but expressed interest in it nonetheless. They gave some idea of what they'd like to see change—adding some depth to the main character, increasing the length, etc.—and offered me an opportunity to revise it and resubmit it. Because the feedback they'd given was useful and meaningful, I spent time tweaking and rewriting, sent it back in, and … they loved it. Even better than the acceptance, though, was that the story had become an overall stronger piece.

"Another time, I received a swift rejection to my application [for] a fellowship with a popular publication. It was the second time I had applied for the annual fellowship, and I was incredibly disappointed. Soon after, a mentor I was working with recommended that I submit a particular story to that same publication (not knowing that I had applied for the fellowship). I was resistant. The story had been included in my application packet, and my feeling was [that] if they hadn't wanted me (and it) for the fellowship, why would they possibly want to publish it? But a friend pointed out that they might be looking for completely different things in fellowship applications than they are in individual stories for publication, so off I sent it. And they accepted it. Had I not tried, tried again, that story wouldn't have found a home with one of my favorite journals.

"All of this is just to say that rejections are not always the downfall we initially see them to be. They can be an opportunity to revise and rethink. The goal is always to grow as a writer, and sending out submissions can get you there, even if it's not quite always through the route you'd expect."

—Denise H. Long

"I have received many rejection notices. Of course, they are never welcome, but any writer who consistently submits material will inevitably experience rejection. However, all is not always lost. One of the more encouraging rejection notices that I have received, among several, was from a mid-tier literary journal where the editor stated that my work did not make the final cut but that [it made it to] the final round of discussion before losing an acceptance vote 3-2. I was specifically asked to submit again. I did so and was happy a few months later to have two pieces accepted by the same journal. Don't give up. Keep writing and submitting. Eventually, good things will happen."

—Dr. Ralph Monday

"A few years ago, I submitted a piece and subsequently received a form rejection via e-mail. Rejection is part of the business; I've no problem with that, but the piece wasn't even removed from the journal's submission queue. This felt particularly insulting. My work deserves a rightful rejection. They've every right to throw the piece in recycling, but I refuse to empty the bin for them. So there it sat in their system for months as a reminder of my stubbornness, my strange sense of writerly pride. And so it remained until a new group of editors came on board, read the piece not knowing it had already been rejected, and sent along another response ... an acceptance."

—Michael Schmeltzer

20

MY BEST WRITING ADVICE

"Writing as a craft is more than a profession and more than a job. It is a love and passion that grips our souls and filters into our day jobs, our families, and our friends. Writing flows from who we are and what we do. When the muse urges, whether it be a piece on child-rearing for a parent magazine or a personal essay about your own growth, answer the call. Don't walk away because that creative spirit inside will wither and move on."

—DR. TRISH DOLASINSKI, E.D.D.

My best advice for someone who wants to see their writing get published is to write often. Find time to fit in as many writing sessions each week as possible. Keep your creativity limber. Practice great opening lines. Play with unusual word combinations. Fill a journal with rants. Do anything to stay engaged with words.

Every writer can make time in his life to write. You don't need to quit your day job. Great bursts of writing can happen fifteen minutes at a time.

Cut back on your television viewing. Shorten your shower in the morning. Use your lunch break to write. Do anything necessary to get a fifteen-minute writing session under your belt once or twice a week. Those fifteen-minute sessions add up fast. Your finished work will pile up, too.

It's just as important to carve out time to read. You need to be an expert in the kind of writing you're producing. Buy a stack of journals. Read a new short story or essay every single day. Absorb the polish of published work. Let other writers' styles encourage you to be original. Get inspired by the amount of great writing being published today.

MAKE FRIENDS

Expand your writing circle by reaching out to writers and editors on Twitter, on Facebook, at conferences, and at your local library. These people, and often the magazines themselves, have social media profiles, making it very easy to find them and connect.

The main social-media players in essay and short-story arenas are Twitter, Facebook, and LinkedIn. Many writers and editors are on Goodreads, Wattpad, Google +, and Pinterest, too, but those sites seem to be more useful for facilitating other kinds of connections—such as those you make with an audience for your book projects. I think the best resource for networking short writing is Twitter, so let's take a look at how to maximize your networking on this platform; then you can recreate the same steps with your Facebook and LinkedIn connections.

Twitter is basically a massive online cocktail party. All you need to do to begin a conversation is to say "hello." On Twitter, a "hello" is when you *follow* someone's feed. Start by following magazines you'd like to know better. Maybe they'll follow you back right away or maybe not. You can either just listen to what they have to say (read their feed), or you can engage with them directly by retweeting their posts or mentioning them in comments. Watch for posts about open submission dates and opportunities. Follow the magazine editors, too. And me, @WindyLynnHarris! I publish freelance opportunities and insider tips every week.

When you retweet someone you'd like to make an authentic connection with, add a personal line or two. Maybe you type "Great blog post!" or "Thank you for the heads-up about that contest." Anything that let's her know you're a professional writer, too, and interested in connecting can only help you.

The goal is to create connections without being annoying, so don't ask a bunch of unsolicited questions and don't pester someone to read your stuff. Instead, read others' work. Support magazines by retweeting their posts. Support writers by retweeting theirs, too. Cheer people on when you can. Congratulate anyone doing anything you think merits applause. When you find a writer publishing stories similar to yours, submit your work to the same magazines. Every time you get a byline, tweet about it. Let the other writers looking for connections know that you're at your desk submitting work, too. Tag the journal in your tweet. Thank them, even. By being part of the literary community, you'll gain an understanding of who appreciates and crafts writing that is stylistically similar to yours.

....

"I intended to join a local writers group, improve craft, [and] network with other writers, but with small kids, life always got in the way: colds, viruses, mounting piles of laundry, exhaustion, the lure of pajamas and a warm laptop in bed ... Then I took an online writing class and met another mom who, like myself, was yearning for connection but didn't have the time to venture out. Together we created WordTango, a writing community for busy writers like ourselves. We soon gained a reputation as an engaging, supportive environment, and writers across the globe joined our online community. Suddenly writing no longer felt isolating. Instead it was a point of connection, a chance for vibrant conversation. I found accountability partners to keep me on track, critique partners to swap stories with, writing buddies to commiserate [with] about rejection and celebrate success. WordTango is like a virtual coffee shop that I can step into ... anytime."

—ELIZABETH PETTIE
....

Visit AWP

Another great way to make connections in the world of short creative writing is to attend the annual AWP Conference & Bookfair. AWP is the Association of Writers & Writing Programs, a literary body that provides support, advocacy, resources, and community to nearly 50,000 writers across the United States. The AWP conference is *the* place to meet journal editors in person. It's the best conference for anyone writing short stories and essays because it is the only conference in the country that features literary magazines and small presses in a big way.

The AWP Bookfair features more than eight-hundred exhibitors, making it the largest marketplace in the country for independent literary presses and journals. Magazines that you've heard of and researched will have a booth there. Visit the magazines you'd like to submit work to, and introduce yourself to the editors. Buy a few copies of their latest issues. Take the time to meet new magazines, too. Ask them what they're looking for in submissions. Shake hands, trade business cards, and most importantly, be yourself. These are your colleagues, people whom you'll want to know for years to come. If you have landed bylines, make a point to visit those magazines that have published you and say, "Thank you!"

With more than 12,000 writers and editors in attendance each year, networking at AWP couldn't be easier. There are panel discussions, readings, presentations, and craft lectures, with journal- and press-sponsored after-parties each night. You'll find terrific connections in the lobby, in the elevator, and waiting in line for the bathroom.

The AWP conference venue changes annually. The next one might be in your area of the country. If you can't attend the conference in person, follow AWP on social media. They'll post information about upcoming events and lots of great moments from the current conference. Visit www.awpwriter.org for more information.

....

"Writing is lonely. Solitary. It's all in your head. I don't know if I could maintain a writing life if I didn't have others, both in real life and on Twitter, with whom I can ask advice and share my

successes and failures. Who else would empathize with me when I gripe that the Harvard Review has let my submission languish in their slush pile for 594 days? Who else will shout 'You go, girl!' when my essay that has been rejected over seventy times finally (hopefully) finds a home?"

—SUSAN LERNER

Go Behind the Scenes

If you'd like to work side-by-side with editors, consider volunteering as a reader for a literary journal. Many are looking for help sorting through their slush pile. Assisting in the selection of submitted work helps you understand what the magazine is looking for, and it gives you a clear view of how publishable contemporary literature reads. You'll gain an inside track to getting published there. It's enjoyable work, even though a lot of it involves saying "no" to people. When you find stand-out work and vote for it to be published, it's a terrific feeling.

You might hear about volunteer opportunities at the magazine's website, but an even easier way to find a magazine open to volunteer positions is to search the journals being published in your state. Send the editor a note saying that you're a local writer looking to learn more about the business. If he doesn't have an opportunity for you, at least you've made a personal connection with an editor whom you can mention by name when you submit your writing to his magazine.

Connect by Having a Blog

There was a time when having a blog felt like a mandatory requirement for writers. Blogs were going to be the new "in" to getting your work noticed. As a result, nearly every writer I knew started a blog. I did, too. Many have stuck with it for nearly a decade. The results for getting work noticed have varied, but all writers will agree that blogs turned out to be a great way to connect with other people writing short fiction and essays. Blogging isn't for everyone and isn't guaranteed to help you find publishing success, but if you're interested in investing time into a blog project, you'll have another great networking avenue in your life.

Blogging 101: An Interview with Rudri Bhatt Patel

Rudri Bhatt Patel is a lawyer turned freelance writer, essayist, and editor. She's also the cofounder and co-editor of *The Sunlight Press*. Her popular site, "Being Rudri," has many regular followers. Rudri is published often with bylines in *The Washington Post, Brain,Child, Literary Mama,* and *ESPN*, to name just a few. She credits her blog as the catalyst for her success. I sat down with Rudri to find out how she got the project started. Here's what she had to say.

WINDY: When did you start your Being Rudri blog, and why did you jump in?

RUDRI: I started Being Rudri in October 2009 as a way to cope with the loss of my father after he fought his four-and-a-half-year battle with cancer. Writing has saved me in a way that I find difficult to explain—I thank my blog for facilitating my journey. My mantra is to negotiate the pendulum between joy and sorrow and to seek contentment. I find my way by writing about this dicey terrain and learning to try to live with uncertainty. Other than my musings on my blog, I write essays and am currently working on a memoir about the Hindu culture and grief and how it provides perspective on life's ordinary graces.

WINDY: What connections have you made by running a blog? Has this ever led to a publishing opportunity?

RUDRI: I've made a tremendous amount of connections with other writers by blogging. Conversations with other writers and exploring online resources have provided me with ongoing confidence to continue to blog and pursue other writing projects. Online publications have looked at my body of work and asked me to write for them, and consequently, many of my paying and nonpaying writing leads were born out of my blog.

WINDY: How can a writer start his own blog today?

RUDRI: Starting a basic blog is easy. These three steps will help you secure a blog:

1. Find a host. There are several places to choose from, but I recommend Blue Host or Go Daddy as potential hosting sites.
2. Secure a domain name. What do you want to call your blog? A domain name is the web address people will type in to access your blog. If you are a writer, I suggest using your full name for your web address.
3. Install WordPress. WordPress is the structure for your blog where you can design your home page, "About Me" page, as well as compose your blog posts.

If you want more thorough instructions, a simple Google search will yield several helpful resources to help you start a blog

WINDY: What should a writer have ready before she begins?

RUDRI: There are several blogs on the web. I'd encourage writers to devise mission statements for their blogs. If you are working on a longer project, do you want your blog to promote that work? Do you want to write about life, writing, reading, or crafts? I recommend narrowing your focus to three interests so you can decide what you want your blog to say about you. Brainstorm before jumping into blog … posts.

Second, writers should devise an "About Me" page to explain why they are blogging and to provide the reader with some background on who they are and what visitors can expect out of the blog. The "About Me" page is usually the second most visited, following the home page.

Third, I'd plan ahead for at least three to five entries to provide a running start for your blog. To keep the momentum going, devise an editorial calendar to plot out your blog posts for every month.

WINDY: What are the dos and don'ts for a writer running a blog?

RUDRI: Your blog is what you decide to make of it. There aren't any rules per se, but if you want to gain confidence and a following, here are a few pointers:

1. Blog consistently.
2. Always focus on writing good content.
3. Make posts about the universal—readers don't want to hear ramblings that sound like a diary entry.
4. Interact with your commenters, and respond to all comments to build a following.
5. Promote your blog on social media.

My Best Writing Advice   227

6. Focus on the writing, not the numbers; this is a process, and blogging is ultimately about improving writing and practicing mindfulness about the practice.

WINDY: How do you get followers?

RUDRI: You build followers through writing good content. People like stories where writers are vulnerable and willing to be authentic. Once readers start frequenting your blog, make certain that you connect with them by answering questions and responding to comments. In addition, building a following requires interacting on social media. I'd recommend Facebook and Twitter as ... starting point[s]. Each writer and blogger has to find the right balance between generating good content and building a following for their work.

WINDY: Is the material you post on your blog considered published?

RUDRI: Most traditional publishing outlets consider pieces on blogs as previously published. With that said, some will consider previously published work for their site. When in doubt, ask or look at the submission guidelines.

WINDY: Can you repost other people's blog posts?

RUDRI: You can repost or cite other people's blog posts as long as you give them credit. Most bloggers might quote a line or two but typically don't repost another blog piece in its entirety on their site.

WINDY: What kinds of topics work best?

RUDRI: Generally, the best topics are the ones [with] which a writer feels a particular kinship. If you don't have a particular affinity for a subject, readers are smart and will pick up on your lack of interest. I'd recommend making a list of topics that interest you and determining their appeal to you and your readers. Universal themes tend to do well in most blogs. Always, though, if the writing is stellar, people will read your work.

WINDY: How often should writers post a new entry? And how long should it be?

RUDRI: For a beginner blog, statistics show that posting three times a week is an ideal schedule. It gives a fair amount of consistency and expectation for the reader. Whatever blogging schedule you choose, make it a routine. To maintain any kind of momentum on a blog, you cannot post pieces erratically. You can build more freedom in your schedule once you get some traction and a devoted following.

BE TENACIOUS

Continue to study your craft year after year. Stay hungry for stronger skills and braver words. Challenge yourself to finish your pieces, and then edit them thoroughly. Share them with other writers and mentors. Accept feedback. Keep working. Polish again.

....

"To me, the main quality for finding success as a writer is tenacity. Not brilliance, not connections, not buckets of available time—though all those things would certainly be nice. But nope, the main quality is tenacity: You must have it to return to the page day after day, year after year. You need it to hone and shape. You certainly need it to 'kill your darlings' and create a story that is as strong as you can build it. But all of that occurs in the comfort of your own world or perhaps with a few close friends. Be tenacious. Keep writing. Art belongs in the world."

—JENNIFER KIRCHER CARR

....

I want you to get published, but it's up to you from here. Joan, Samantha, Hershel, and I (and thousands of other writers out there) are working on short stories and essays this week. We'll be editing and polishing and rewriting our work until it's ready. We'll be finding potential markets and tidying up our pages. We'll be sucking in our breath and sending out our work, hoping to hear good things. We'll be cheering each other on and lifting each other up, learning together and growing in our craft. You can be part of all this, too. I invite you to join the fun.

APPENDIX: THE STEP-BY-STEP SUBMISSION PLAN

STEP ONE: CATEGORIZE YOUR WORK

Short Story Categorization

1. What is your word count? Remember: Word count for short writing means the words on the page without the title or byline.
2. Based on the word count, is this story microfiction? Flash fiction? Or is it best described as a short story?
3. Is this a genre or literary short story? If it's a genre story, what genre is it?
4. What subcategories can you identify? Ex: historical, humor, romance, LGBTQ, religious
5. What topics can you identify in this story? List as many as you can. Ex: marriage, grief, dog shelters, antique cars, restaurants, the environment.

Personal Essay Categorization

1. What is your word count? Remember: Essay word count only reflects the body of your essay. Don't count your title or subtitle.
2. Which main category of essay did you write? Literary, reported, or "other"?
3. Is this essay a piece of creative nonfiction?
4. What subcategories can you identify in your piece? Did you write a narrative essay? A travel essay? Political? Parenting?
5. Finally, what topics does your essay contain? Identify as many as you can. Ex: mental illness, sailing, safety, seasons, history, sports.

STEP TWO: FIND POTENTIAL MARKETS

Begin your market research by opening the pages of *Writer's Market* or going online to Duotrope, *The Review Review*, or *Poets & Writers*. Read a magazine's writers' guidelines thoroughly, and refer to your category list to make a sincere match. Keep working until you have five viable options.

STEP THREE: WRITE A COVER LETTER

Write a great cover letter to a specific editor for a specific reason. Remember to say:

1. "Hello"
2. "Here's What I'm Sending You"
3. "Here's Who I Am"
4. "Thank You"

Use this example as a guide:

> Dear Mr. Bailey:
>
> I'm submitting my 100-word flash-fiction story, "Everyone Says So," for your consideration. I am sending you this story because I read in

the writers' guidelines that you're looking for writing that bridges the gap between dream and reality.

My work has been published in *The Literary Review, 34thParallel*, and *Poor Mojo's Almanac(k)*, among many other journals.

Thank you for your time. I look forward to hearing from you.

Sincerely,
Fabulous Writer

STEP FOUR: FORMAT YOUR MANUSCRIPT

1. Print your manuscript on 8 ½" x 11" white paper (use only one side of the paper).
2. Use 1 to 1-½" margins all around.
3. Use twelve-point standard typeface: Times New Roman or Courier (no fancy script).
4. Do not use end-of-the-line hyphenated words or justified right margins.
5. Double-space the entire manuscript.
6. Indent paragraphs five spaces (this is the preset on your "tab" button).
7. Do not use additional spacing between paragraphs.

Next, add identifying information, your byline, and the header:

8. Type your name, address, phone number, and e-mail address in the upper-left corner, single-spaced. In the upper-right corner, type the word count. You can round the word count up to the nearest hundred or the nearest ten in short pieces if you'd like. If you're writing under a pen name, place your real name (the person you want the check made out to) in the top-left corner on the first page. Use your pen name as your byline underneath the title. It's always a good idea to mention in your cover letter that you use a pen name.
9. Drop down about halfway on the first page, and center your title. Your byline goes beneath it. These are double-spaced.
10. On page two (and subsequent pages), add a header that includes your title and last name.

11. Be sure to double-check your page numbers and headers. They need to be in the same font as the rest of your manuscript.

STEP FIVE: SUBMIT LIKE A PRO!

When you're ready to take the last step, reread the magazine's writers' guidelines for instructions, and follow them exactly. Watch for the words "simultaneous submissions" and "multiple submissions." If the magazine accepts simultaneous submissions, you can send the same piece to several magazines at the same time. If the magazine accepts multiple submissions, you can send the magazine more than one of your pieces at the time of submission. Stay organized by recording your submission in a tracker of some kind. Be brave; you're a professional writer. Take a deep breath, and send in that work!

Snail Mail Submission

1. Paperclip the pages of your manuscript together. Never use staples (editors need to make quick copies of your manuscript for editorial boards).
2. Fold your SASE (self-addressed stamped envelope) into thirds and tuck it behind your manuscript, under the paperclip. The SASE is addressed to *you*. Write the magazine's address in the top-left corner, and attach a stamp.
3. Place your signed cover letter on top of the manuscript. Remember to sign your name at the bottom.
4. Fewer than five pages can be folded into a standard business envelope. Five pages or more should be mailed flat in a manila envelope.
5. Mail your manuscripts first class (with a regular stamp). Never certify or register a submission.

E-Mail Submission

1. Begin the e-mail message with your cover letter, minus your contact information.

2. Include your manuscript's text in the e-mail's body, below the cover letter (unless the writers' guidelines specifically asked for manuscripts to be sent as an attachment, which is rare).

3. In the subject line, write the words "Query: Title of Your Story." If the magazine's writers' guidelines give you other instructions, follow those instead. Some ask that you specify fiction or nonfiction in the subject line.

Digital Upload Submission

All uploads have an online form that give you a place to enter your contact information and cover letter. You do not need to change your cover letter to a Word file or PDF; just copy and paste it into the correct box. Your manuscript does need to be a Word file or a PDF. When you select the option to upload your work, you will be able to select the correct file type.

CONTRIBUTORS

BREE BARTON has published short fiction in *The Iowa Review, Mid-American Review,* and Roxane Gay's *PANK.* Her nonfiction has appeared in *USA Today, Los Angeles Times,* and *McSweeney's,* and her face has appeared in a couple of web series you've probably never seen. Her debut novel, *Heart of Thorns,* is forthcoming from Katherine Tegen/HarperCollins in 2018. She's also an editor, ghostwriter, dance teacher, improviser, and (she hopes) a decent human being. You can visit her online at www.breebarton.com.

RUDRI BHATT PATEL is a lawyer turned writer and editor. Prior to attending law school, she graduated with an MA in English and an emphasis in creative writing. She is cofounder and co-editor of *The Sunlight Press* and on staff at *Literary Mama.* Her work has appeared in *The Washington Post, Brain, Child, ESPN, Role Reboot, Mothers Always Write, The First Day, Parent.co, Raising Arizona Kids,* and elsewhere. She is currently working on a memoir on grief, the Hindu culture, and how it provides perspective on life's ordinary graces. She lives in Arizona with her family. You can visit her online at www.beingrudri.com.

APRIL BRADLEY is from Goodlettsville, Tennessee, and lives with her family on the Connecticut shoreline near New Haven. Her writing has appeared in *Blue Fifth Review, Flash Frontier, Hermeneutic Chaos Literary Journal, The Journal of Compressed Creative*

Arts, Narratively, NANO Fiction, and *Thrice Fiction,* among others. She has a Master's in Ethics from Yale University and studied philosophy and theology as a post-graduate scholar at Cambridge University. Her fiction has been nominated for the *Best of the Net* Anthology and for the 2017 Pushcart Prize. She is the associate editor for *Bartleby Snopes* and the founder and editor of *Women Who Flash Their Lit.* She also is a resident writing coach at Writers Helping Writers. Find her stumbling through digital space at www.aprilbradley.net.

CHELSEY CLAMMER is the author of *BodyHome* and winner of the 2015 Red Hen Press Nonfiction Manuscript Award for her essay collection, *Circadian.* She has been published in *The Rumpus, Hobart, McSweeney's,* and *Black Warrior Review,* among others. She is the essays editor for *The Nervous Breakdown* and a volunteer reader for *Creative Nonfiction.* She teaches creative writing online with *WOW! Women on Writing* and received her MFA from The Rainier Writing Workshop. You can visit her online at www.chelseyclammer.com.

DR. TRISH DOLASINSKI, ED.D. is a freelance writer and editor. She also instructs doctoral candidates at Grand Canyon University in Arizona. An educator for more than thirty years, she has taught elementary and middle-school students, as well as graduate students at two major universities. Trish is currently in the final revision stages of her first novel. She lives in Scottsdale, AZ, with her husband and enjoys her eight grandchildren. You can visit her online at www. trishdolasinskiwrites.com.

KATHY FISH teaches flash fiction for the Mile High MFA program at Regis University in Denver. She has published four collections of short fiction: a chapbook in the Rose Metal Press collective, *A Peculiar Feeling of Restlessness: Four Chapbooks of Short Short Fiction by Four Women* (2008), *Wild Life* (Matter Press, 2011), *Together We Can Bury It* (The Lit Pub, 2012), and *Rift,* co-authored with Robert Vaughan (Unknown Press, 2015). Her story, "A Room With Many Small Beds," was chosen by Stuart Dybek for inclusion in *The Best Small Fictions 2016* (Queen's Ferry Press). You can visit her online at www.kathy-fish.com.

LISA FUGARD is the author of the award-winning novel *Skinner's Drift* and *21 Days to Awaken the Writer Within*. She has written frequently for the *New York Times* travel section. Her short story "Night Calls" is anthologized in a school textbook published by Houghton Mifflin Harcourt, and she loves the e-mails she gets from ninth graders asking about her story's symbolism. She lives in southern California where she writes and mentors those interested in learning more about a writer's craft. You can visit her online at www.lisafugard.com.

STUART HORWITZ is a ghostwriter, independent editor, and founder of Book Architecture (www.bookarchitecture.com), a firm of independent editors whose clients have reached the best-seller list in both fiction and nonfiction and have appeared on *Oprah*, *the TODAY Show*, *The Tonight Show*, and in the most prestigious journals in their respective fields. He is the author of three books on writing: *Blueprint Your Bestseller: Organize and Revise Any Manuscript With the Book Architecture Method*, which was named one of 2013's best books about writing by *The Writer*; *Book Architecture: How to Plot and Outline Without Using a Formula* (2015), which became an Amazon bestseller; and *Finish Your Book in Three Drafts: How to Write a Book, Revise a Book, and Complete a Book While You Still Love It* (2016).

ALICE KALTMAN is the author of the story collection *Staggerwing* (Tortoise Books) and the forthcoming novel *Wavehouse* (Fitzroy Books 2018). Her work has also appeared in numerous journals including *Hobart*, *Whiskeypaper*, *Storychord*, and *Joyland*, and in the anthologies *The Pleasure You Suffer* and *On Montauk: A Literary Celebration*. She lives, writes, and surfs in Brooklyn and Montauk, New York. You can visit her online at www.alicekaltman.com.

JENNIFER KIRCHER CARR is a writer living in western New York. Her fiction has been published in numerous literary journals, including *Prairie Schooner*, *Alaska Quarterly Review*, *The Rumpus*, *Storyscape Literary Journal*, *North American Review*, and *The Nebraska Review*, which awarded her the Fiction Prize. Her nonfiction has been published in *Poets & Writers*, *Ploughshares* blog, and *Edible Finger Lakes*, among others. She is co-curator at WordTango, an online community for writers. Her works in progress include a novel and a collection of linked stories. You can visit her online at www.jenniferkirchercarr.com.

BRIANNE M. KOHL's short stories have appeared in several publications, including *The Masters Review, The Stoneslide Corrective, Literary Mama, The Bohemyth, Coup d'Etat,* and *Menda City Review.* She has published several tips articles and interviews at *The Review Review.* To see all of her publications and awards, visit her at www.briannekohl.com. Follow her at twitter.com/BrianneKohl.

DR. MICHELLE LEE is an English professor at Daytona State College. She has edited various academic and literary journals, has been nominated for a Pushcart Prize, and has published across genres. You can find her most recent work in the anthology *All We Can Hold* by Sage Hill Press and with *Hypertrophic Literary,* as well as online with *Toasted Cheese Literary Journal* and *Spry Literary Journal.* You can email her at michelle.lee@daytonastate.edu.

SUSAN LERNER is a student in Butler's MFA in Creative Writing program. She reads for *Booth: A Journal,* which also published her interview with Jonathan Franzen. Her work has appeared in *The Rumpus, The Believer Logger, Front Porch Journal, Atticus Review, Literary Mama,* and elsewhere. Susan's essay "Only A Memory" was a finalist for the *Crab Orchard Review*'s 2016 Rafael Torch Literary Nonfiction Award. Susan lives in Indianapolis.

JEANNE LYET GASSMAN's debut novel, *Blood of a Stone* (Tuscany Press), received a 2015 Independent Publisher Book Award (bronze) in the national category of religious fiction and was a finalist for the New Mexico-Arizona Book Awards and the 2015 Independent Author Network Book of the Year Award. Her short work has been nominated for Queen's Ferry Press's Best Small Fictions series and the Pushcart Prize. Additional awards include fellowships from Ragdale and the Arizona Commission on the Arts. Jeanne's short stories and creative nonfiction have appeared in *Queen Mob's Tea House, Hippocampus Magazine,*

Altarwork, Hermeneutic Chaos Literary Journal, Literary Mama, Red Savina Review, Switchback, Barrelhouse, and *The Museum of Americana,* among many others. Her short story, "Sweet Dirty Love," is included in the anthology *Debris & Detritus: The Lesser Greek Gods Running Amok.* You can visit her online at www.jeannelyetgassman.com.

JOLENE MCILWAIN is a part-time lecturer at Chatham and Duquesne Universities, focusing on literary theory and creative and argumentative writing. Her fiction has been nominated for a Pushcart Prize and twice selected finalist in *Glimmer Train*'s contests. Her work appears in *Prairie Schooner* (online), *River Teeth* (online), *The Fourth River, JOCCA's* www.flashfiction.net, *Prime Number Magazine,* and elsewhere. She's the recipient of an artist grant from the Greater Pittsburgh Arts Council and is currently working on a collection of short fiction and a novel set in the hills of western Pennsylvania's Appalachian plateau. She is an associate flash fiction editor at *jmww.*

DR. RALPH MONDAY is a professor of English at Roane State Community College in Harriman, TN, and has published hundreds of poems in more than one-hundred journals. A chapbook, *All American Girl and Other Poems,* was published in July 2014. A book, *Empty Houses and American Renditions,* was published in May 2015 by Aldrich Press. A Kindle chapbook, *Narcissus the Sorcerer,* was published in June 2015 by Odin Hill Press. An e-book, *Bergman's Island & Other Poems,* was published by *Poetry Repairs* in March 2017, and a humanities text is scheduled for publication by Kendall Hunt in 2018. You can visit him online at www.ralphmonday.com.

DENISE HOWARD LONG's short fiction has appeared in *SmokeLong Quarterly, Pithead Chapel, The Journal of Compressed Creative Arts, The Tishman Review, The Evansville Review,* and elsewhere. Denise lives in Nebraska with her husband and two young sons. You can visit her online at www.denisehlong.com.

LYNN O'ROURKE HAYES is a writer, photographer, and passionate traveler. Her adventures have taken her to more than one-hundred countries on six continents, across deserts, down rivers, over mountains, under the sea, through jungles, and to fourty-eight of our fifty states. She writes a syndicated column for the *Dallas Morning News's site* and shares stories on her site www.familytravel.com. When not traveling, she splits her time between Scottsdale, AZ, and Whitefish, MT. You can visit her online at www.lynnorourkehayes.com.

ELIZABETH PETTIE is co-founder of the online writing community WordTango, which hosts writing classes, a networking group, and online writing events for busy writers such as herself. She finds time for her own writing after dark and during her daughter's naps. She has a passion for children's literature but is currently following the write-what-you-know advice and is at work on a novel for adults about a frazzled mom of two small girls who's house is coated in a layer of crushed bunny crackers and Cheerios. You can visit her online at www. elizabethpettie.com.

SUSAN POHLMAN is the author of *Halfway to Each Other: How a Year in Italy Brought Our Family Home.* She won the Relationships category and was the runner-up in the Memoirs category in the 2010 Next Generation Indie Book Awards. Her essays have been published in a variety of print and online publications, including *The Washington Times, Guideposts, Homelife, Good Housekeeping* (online), *Erma Bombeck Writers' Workshop, The Review Review,* and *The Mid.* She teaches creative writing in small-group settings, speaks at conferences, and hosts an annual writing retreat in Santa Fe, NM. You can visit her online at www.susanpohlman.com.

MICHAEL SCHMELTZER was born in Yokosuka, Japan, and eventually moved to the United States. He is the author of *Elegy/Elk River* (Floating Bridge Press, 2015), winner of the Floating Bridge Press Chapbook Award, and *Blood Song* (Two Sylvias Press, 2016), which was longlisted for the Julie Suk Award. A debut nonfiction book, *A Single Throat Opens* (a lyric exploration of addiction written collaboratively with Meghan McClure), is forthcoming from Black Lawrence Press. You can visit him online at www.michaelschmeltzer.com.

SAVANNAH THORNE graduated from the University of Iowa, where she studied in the Writers' Workshop under many of poetry's great voices. She also holds cum laude Master's degrees from DePaul University in Chicago and Norwich University in Northfield, Vermont. Her poetry has appeared in more than thirty literary journals. Her fiction is represented by the Linda Chester Literary Agency. You can visit her online at www.savvyedit.com.

BECKY TUCH is the founding editor of *The Review Review*, a website that has been listed for the past six years in *Writer's Digest's* 101 Best Websites for Writers. Becky's fiction has won awards from *Moment*, *Glimmer Train*, *The Briar Cliff Review*, and elsewhere. Other writing has appeared in *Salon*, *Virginia Quarterly Review* (online), *Salt Hill*, *Cleaver, Graze, Hobart, Eclipse, Folio, Night Train,* and more. She has received literature fellowships from The MacDowell Colony and the Somerville Arts Council. Currently, she lives in Pittsburgh. You can visit her online at www.beckytuch.com.

HILLARY UMLAND comes from a long line of writers and artists. She is a writer living and working in Nebraska. You can find Hillary's work in *Unbroken* and *Sick Lit Magazine*.

INDEX

WD WRITER'S DIGEST